MEMO

BOMB DISPOSAL MAN

208

BOMB DISPOSAL

T.N.T.

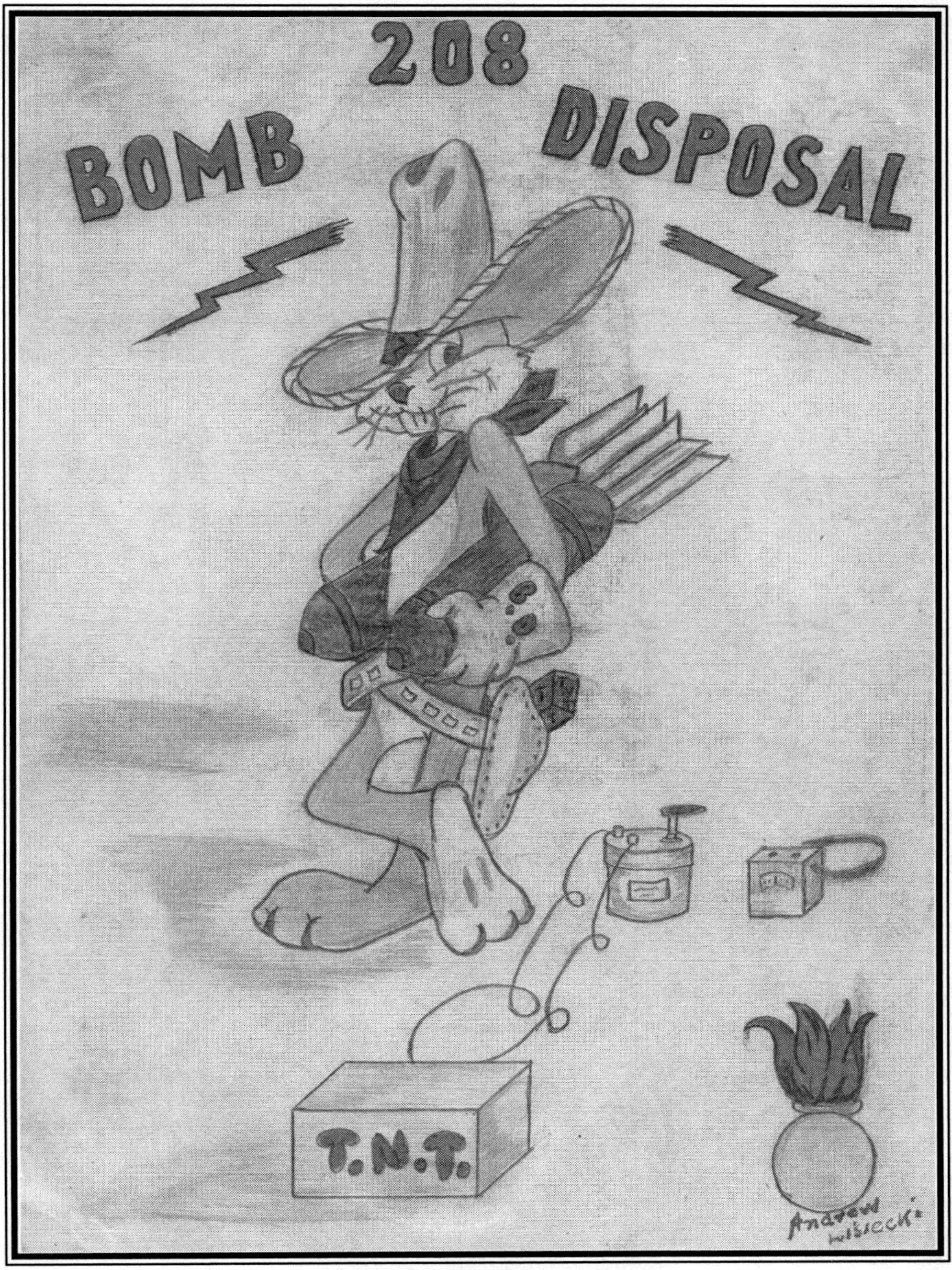

BY WIN FIRMAN

DEAR LEE —

GOOD TO MEET YOU! HAVE

A GREAT LIFE.

WARM REGARDS

Design & layout by Ted Slawski

ISBN # 0-9678570-7-7
printed by Lightening Source Inc.
La Vergne, Tennessee U.S.A.

TABLE OF CONTENTS

Lieutenant Win Firman

PREFACE

Once upon a time, long, long ago, a young man dreamed of battles he would fight, a maiden he would wed, and children he would sire to carry on his legacy. He lived his early years laying the groundwork for a life of service and love. This is a key part of his story.

Now in his nineties, married to his high school sweetheart for nearly seventy years and with his three children in their sixties, he can look back in satisfaction at the life fate chose for him.

World War II would have a huge impact on his character, as it did for millions of other young men and women. Here he underwent a life and death struggle while separated from his young family. Good fortune was on his side and he lived to write this story of those defining years. Yes, there are a host of other stories in the years that Julie and Win have had together, but their children and grandchildren know those stories, lived many of them. The lonely life of a bomb disposal man, they could not know. So here it is—from memories of a time seventy years ago.

SELECTIVE SERVICE SYSTEM

SELECTIVE SERVICE
LOCAL BOARD #743
SCARSDALE, N.Y.

(STAMP OF LOCAL BOARD)

March 20, 1941

Mr. Winfield Firman
Delta Upsilon Fraternity
Amherst College
Amherst, Massachusetts

Dear Win:-

I was tickled to death to receive your letter of March 17 and I am very glad to write a letter of recommendation for you which I am enclosing.

I was very much interested when I heard of your engagement to Miss Fisher and I am sure you will both be very happy.

I really hope your eyes will not cause you to be rejected by the draft as I feel that not only would you get a great deal out of a year's service in the army but I also feel that you could contribute a lot to the country in this line.

I trust that the next time you are in Scarsdale, you will get in touch with me and come down and see your old troop.

With congratulations to you and best wishes to Miss Fisher, I am

Sincerely yours,

Kevney O'Connor

Kevney O'Connor

The person named herein whose Order No. is 728
Has been classified by {Local Board / Board of Appeals}
in Class I-A until - (Date)
Member of Local Board.
Notify your employer of this classification 7/2/41 (Date)
This card may be cut on dotted line for convenience in carrying.
D. S. S. Form 57
14 (A-22287)
REGISTRANT—SIGN HERE
Winfield Firman

Chapter One

A SHORT HISTORY OF WORLD WAR II BOMB DISPOSAL

The British, who declared war on Germany in 1939, were unprepared for the onslaught of German bombs as "The Battle of Britain" began in 1940. Thousands of bombs rained on England and particularly London and a significant number of those bombs did not explode. The U.S. Ordnance Manual on exploded bombs estimates 5-10% of bombs dropped did not explode becoming UXBs—unexploded bombs. Some of these were duds, but perhaps 75% were armed with time-delay fuzes[1], set to go off in one to forty-eight hours—some even longer.

Obviously these hundreds and hundreds of bombs represented a real threat to the civilian population as well as to buildings and utilities.

At first, the hazardous task of removing these bombs was given to the British Army Royal Engineers. They were untrained and casualties, as one would expect, were high. To obviate this unskilled approach to dealing with UXBs, the British army began dragooning officers, and later enlisted men, into the first bomb disposal groups. The Royal Engineers founded the first formal bomb disposal school in late 1941.

Much of the early training in how to render bombs inert was

1. The bomb fuze, unlike the electrical fuse in your closet, was a device with a highly sensitive and volatile explosive such as mercury fulminate or lead azide, which, on impact, would create enough of an explosion to detonate the bomb.

"by guess and by God," and for the lack of better understanding of bomb disposal, the casualties continued to be high. At first, the newly designated bomb disposal personnel followed a rather routine procedure—dig up the UXB, apply a pipe wrench to the fuze, twist it a few times in order to remove and Lo! And Behold! The bomb is inert.

Most of the bombs used by the allies, Germans and Italians, were a large block of TNT or Amatol (the Japanese used Picric Acid) and all of these are relatively insensitive. A TNT bomb can drop thousands of feet and, absent a fuze, not explode on impact, though it can explode in a fire.

So, if the fuze is successfully removed, the bomb is inert and can be tossed into the back of a truck and taken some place for disposal—often at sea but frequently blown up in a deserted area. The British bomb disposal men quickly learned techniques of safely extracting fuzes including several ways of stopping clockwork or time delay fuzes.

Unfortunately, the British newspapers made too much of the bomb disposal troops. One showed a huge German bomb hanging like a large tuna from a tripod while the proud B.D. officer looked on. The British newspapers were, of course, regularly received in Germany and read...so the Germans determined they would make the task of the bomb disposal troops more dangerous by booby-trapping the fuzes in their bombs. They came up with one booby trap called the Zeus 40, which was a fuze put under the main bomb fuze. The main bomb fuze, which was 10 or 12 inches long, and about 2.5 inches in diameter and rather looked like a piston, was pushed down into the Zeus 40, which had a spring loaded striker, and the principal fuze held this back from the primer, until, of course, the main fuze was removed. Then, the spring-loaded striker went into the primer, set off the fuze, set off the bomb, and killed the bomb disposal officer removing it.

The British had no idea what was happening as officer after officer was killed. One lucky day, a Zeus 40 did not function and the bomb disposal officer looked down and saw death staring him in the face. They now knew they had to take steps to combat this new threat to their bomb disposal techniques. This became a cat and mouse game throughout the war with the British overcoming German ingenuity and the Germans creating more and more problems for British bomb disposal.

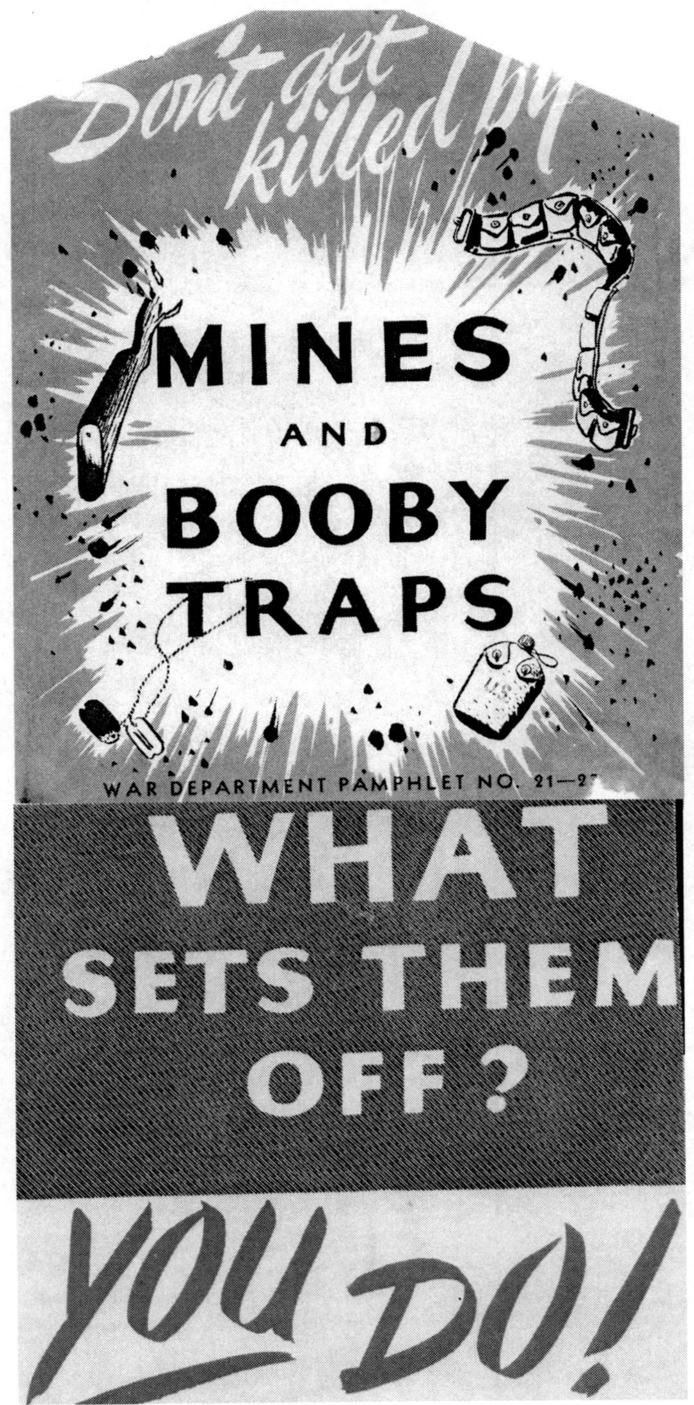
Don't get killed by
MINES
AND
BOOBY
TRAPS
WAR DEPARTMENT PAMPHLET NO. 21—2
WHAT
SETS THEM
OFF?
YOU DO!

Devastation of German bombs in Europe

Chapter Two

THE UNITED STATES ENTERS THE WAR

So now, let us fast forward to December 7 1941, when the Japanese attacked Pearl Harbor. President Roosevelt gave a stirring speech before Congress and persuaded an almost unanimous Congress (one Senator took an opposing stance) to declare war on Japan on December 8. A few days thereafter, Germany declared war on the U.S. and we were involved on two fronts. The U.S. army was now in bomb disposal, something with which they had no experience, as had been the case with the British earlier. Not only UXBs, but artillery shells, land mines, and booby-traps were the purview of the newly formed U.S. bomb disposal companies and squads. Naval mines fell to specially trained navy mine disposal personnel. The newly created bomb disposal section started off by training officers at the Aberdeen Proving Grounds in Maryland, and set out to deal with German bombs, obviously not in the continental U.S., but in England and, subsequently, France. Japanese bombs were dealt with on the islands in the Pacific. Surprisingly, there were also a large number of U.S. bombs that did not explode on impact and became part of the problem. Fortunately, we had all of the hard-won experience of the British bomb disposal groups to help us understand these problems and how to deal with them, so that we did not have to employ the trial and error method, which had been so costly to the personnel of the British bomb disposal units.

A viewing of the five-part, British, fictional film, *Danger: UXB* clearly illustrates the trial and error methods used in early B.D. work. This film so accurately depicted many of the techniques of dealing with these explosives that it reflects, even to this day, the intricacies of bomb disposal.

In January 1942, the U.S. bomb disposal school was created by the Ordnance Department at Aberdeen Proving Grounds. The school's commander and his staff brought back equipment and techniques from England, as it was the most advanced and immediate information that was available at that time. This was the material for early training of bomb disposal officers at the beginning of World War II.

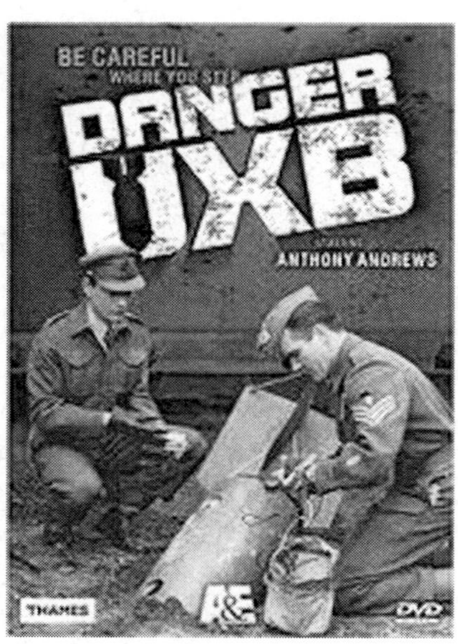

Chapter Three

A BIT OF PERSONAL HISTORY

Julie Fisher and I had held hands through Scarsdale High School and while she was attending Sweet Briar College in Virginia and I, Amherst College in Massachusetts. At the prom in our Junior year of college, I proposed to her, and she happily accepted. Of course, the question of when we might be married came up immediately. At first, we considered a year from graduation so that I could become established in business, but, as the war clouds loomed in my senior year, we decided to bring it down to six months after graduation, which would have fallen right about the time of Pearl Harbor. But, as Julie said, "If we're going to do it in December, why not in June? And then if the war catches you, we'll have time together before you go off into the army." So, it was agreed that we would be married the week before commencement. A small side note: I broke my ankle playing softball a month before we were to be married, but Julie laughingly said that was no excuse and the marriage would proceed. Which it did. And we were married June 7th, 1941 in Julie's hometown of Scarsdale, New York, attended by all the family from both sides. This included my three brothers and my father, who shall show up again later in this story. We returned to Amherst from Atlantic City, where we honeymooned, so that I could attend my graduation ceremonies.

I still have the receipt from our seven-day stay at Colton Manor on the boardwalk in Atlantic City. The hotel was on the American Plan (three meals a day included in the room fee), so we enjoyed twenty-one excellent meals, often steak or lobster, a large and beautiful double room with fresh flowers for the honeymooners—and the tab?—$70.05. I was never told what the nickel was for, but who could complain? As Archie and Edith Bunker would sing many years later, "Those were the days." Marriage, honeymoon, graduation from college and entrance into the military. Much happened in a short time.

The newlyweds & their parents: celebrating a marriage, preparing for war

Chapter Four

THE WAR COMES HOME

Again, fast forward: I was not drafted because of my marital status, but I was very determined that I would do my share in the war so that, even with a small child, I became a volunteer officer candidate. This option was for people with financial responsibilities who could not, perhaps, afford to enlist. The volunteer officer candidates were guaranteed a chance to go to officer candidate school and I was chosen to go to Camp Davis in North Carolina, which was the Anti-Aircraft Officer Candidate School, after I had completed basic training at Fort Eustis, the Coast Artillery Replacement Training Center. At Camp Upton, on Long Island, where I started out, had hundreds of draftees waiting to be sent to one of the many camps in the country for basic training. How do you keep them busy after a little close order drill and instruction on the care and assembly of the Garand and Springfield rifles? Answer: have tons of cement blocks which need to be moved 100 yards away in the morning and returned to their original location in the afternoon. The most well-traveled cement blocks in history.

The food was pretty bad and served to the G.I. by bored K.P's with big spoons. "Just a little." SPLAT! "None of that!" SPLOSH! More than could be eaten if it HAD been good! But an officer at the garbage cans refused to let anyone dump food. (Were the Chinese starving?) So we would scrape the glop into our fatigue pockets and dump it into the woods when we got by "Eagle Eye." Didn't really do much for our fatigues.

After a few days of indoctrination at Camp Upton (which I would not recommend for anyone) I was transferred to Battery D, at Fort Eustis, Virginia. Basic training took thirteen weeks and was a heavy dose of close order drill, firing and cleaning 40 mm cannon, long hikes (up to twenty miles) along with K.P., inspections and harassment from cadre. We were trained to fire Springfield and Garand rifles (I qualified as "expert"), carbines which were short barreled light rifles ("sharpshooter") and .45 caliber pistols (my best was only "marksmen"). The standard army sidearm was the .38 caliber pistol until the Philippine insurrection when the .38 didn't even slow a drug sodden Moro tribesman. The .45 will stop a water buffalo at close range, but due to its heavy recoil, is difficult to shoot with accuracy.

While I was taking basic training there, Camp Davis was shut down along with its anti-aircraft officer candidate school because we suddenly had more anti-aircraft officers than the army really needed. I, therefore, was on the horns of a dilemma: I could take a discharge from the army because they could not fulfill their pledge to send me to officer candidate school, or I could waive my rights to officer candidate school, and stay on in the army. What would have happened if I were to have accepted a discharge from the army? I was told that I would probably be drafted within a month or two and sent back for basic training someplace else. With this unappetizing "Hobson's" choice I decided to stay on in the army and was made a corporal in the anti-aircraft battalion. All of our training was on 40 mm anti-aircraft guns, which were also considered to be useful anti-tank guns. These guns were especially useful on naval ships against low flying aircraft. But they were completely useless against the armor of the German Tiger tanks where the shells would bounce off harmlessly. Ultimately the U.S. Army went to 90 mm guns for anti-tank purposes.

When it appeared I was going to be permanent cadre in a stateside A.A. Battalion, Julie and I made plans to live together (with daughter Frances, just over 10 months old). We found some tiny concrete homes in Newport News, perhaps 20 miles from Fort Eustis. The price was right, probably $20.00 a month and as two of our sergeants lived in this little development transportation was not a problem.

SCARSDALE, NEW YORK — FRIDAY, JANUARY 28, 1944

Furlough

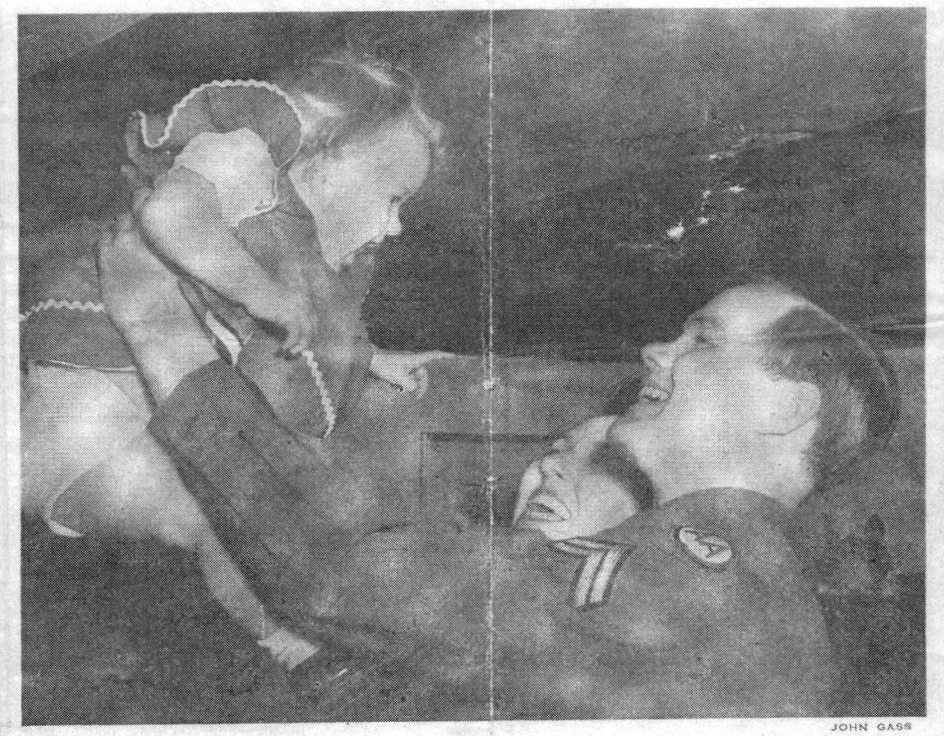

JOHN GASS

Corporal Winfield Firman of the Army found his hands full with his young daughter, Frances Ann, who has reached the age of one year in a cheerful sort of way, during his furlough. He left yesterday for Aberdeen, Maryland, where he is assigned to Ordnance. Mrs. Firman, looking on, is the former Miss Juliet Fisher of Circle Road.

Married and off to war

Chapter Five

OUR YOUNG FAMILY

I was, of course, in the military and at camp daily, but we still had a rich, playful family life. In spite of being relatively poor, we were in love and lived in a community of people in similar circumstances. It is hard to imagine enjoying a happy life while preparing to go to war, but in fact we had one. Being young helped, as we had an old-fashioned ice box (40 pounds of ice delivered weekly), a coal stove (so our own crawling child was always covered in coal dust—quite a sight), and paper thin walls. Sounds between apartments were easily heard. I don't know what our neighbors would remember of what went on in our home, but we have some fond and funny memories. Almost daily, from next door would come a voice saying, "Lena Delores, you peed in the bed!" The little girl who played with our little girl was (apparently) being toilet trained. And, more amusing still were the two sergeants who would knock on their common wall when they began with their wives and the first done would knock triumphantly.

Over Christmas, Julie and her neighbor decided to make fruit cake, using Francie's little enamel bathtub: a pound of this, a pound of that, a quart of this, a pint of that, nuts, dried fruit, and there it was: sixty pounds of fruitcake—I kid you not! Not easy to give away (or eat) your thirty pounds and after a while we loathed the sight of fruitcake. To this day I rarely eat it and Julie has never made it again.

Julie's family had lent us a Ford convertible while we were stationed at Fort Eustis. It was a fairly late model, but the tires were bald and new tires, in wartime, were impossible to get. The top sergeant in our company had wrangled four new tires for his old wreck which he was selling. He came to us with a cool proposition: "Lend me your convertible for my vacation and I will swap the tires on the two cars." Of course, we jumped at the offer and wound up with a set of nearly new tires. There is no record of what the man, who was buying the sergeant's old car, thought when he saw the bald tires rather than the new ones he had bargained for.

Old car, new tires!

Chapter Six

THE BEGINNING OF MY BOMB DISPOSAL CAREER

Subsequently, perhaps due to the good offices of my father, who was on the War Production Board in Washington, and mingled with many high officers and their wives, I was given an assignment to OCS at Aberdeen Proving Grounds in Maryland, where I began a four-month officer candidate training program. Officer candidate school was not much of an ordeal after basic training. Class I-62 (mine) lost about twelve aspiring officers, who washed out of a class of about sixty. Many had difficulty with "voice and command"—the ability to drill troops—and night after night we would hear them on the parade grounds drilling an imaginary platoon: "To the rear *HARCH*, by the left flank *HARCH*, platoon *HALT*!"

We had a fair amount of classroom instruction. In these we were seated alphabetically. One of our instructors had a problem with names, so "Firman followed by Fosberg" became "Firberg and Fosman." A name I carried to graduation.

Maryland in winter (January '44) is cold! We candidates kept wood stoves burning all night in our barracks to keep us and the pipes from freezing. This, it seems, was too easy for us, so only a campout would do. In the field, we encountered tear gas bombs for gas mask training, long hikes

through the snow and frozen butts from our outdoor latrines. The military school graduates in the class sure could make a tight bed—drop a quarter on it and it would bounce in the air—but sleeping in freezing weather in pup tents had been no part of their training, so they slept little. A sergeant, back from the European Theater, and I found a discarded 20 pound tin in which we punched holes, inverted it and built a wood fire in it between the two halves of our pup tent and slept the night away.

The final exercise for our class was a simulated invasion. The target—a flag—inland a few hundred yards, with a line of huts, guarded by our cadre, who needed to be taken out to get to the objective. I was assigned the post of C.O. of the invasion—an undesirable assignment which could wash one out if handled badly.

At 5:00 AM we boarded landing craft and headed for the "enemy" troops. We had heavily fortified chocolate bars that were the equivalent of three meals. "Caution: Eat only 1/3 of the bar every 3-4 hours." But they were tasty and some of the men gobbled them down only to become very sick in a very short time. Out into the cold water from the landing craft, rifles held high. The typical group in this exercise cleaned out the "enemy" in the huts first, taking half an hour, before heading for the flag. I had troops isolating the defenders while half of us drove straight for the flag. Surprise! The officers with the flag didn't expect us for another thirty minutes and were eating and smoking, with their rifles stacked, when we burst in on them. I must have passed the test with flying colors because at graduation a few days later, I was assigned as a platoon leader, one of the top three posts.

Julie had come down from Scarsdale for the graduation of my class, and to pin my new bars on and Dad, newly commissioned in the Navy, was there to receive my first salute. A glorious day! At the conclusion of our training program and, as we emerged brand new second lieutenants in the Army of the United States, we were faced with a choice of what branch of the ordnance service we would choose to go into. Our choices on graduation were fire control, tank recovery, medium maintenance, heavy maintenance, small arms, and perhaps some others that I don't re-

ARMY SERVICE FORCES
ORDNANCE DEPARTMENT
THE ORDNANCE SCHOOL
ABERDEEN PROVING GROUND, MD.

TO INSURE PROMPT ATTENTION IN REPLY REFER TO

______ NO. ______

ATTENTION OF

______

27 May 1944

Subject: Temporary Appointment.

To: 2nd Lt. FIRMAN, WILFIELD A 01 558 456
Army of the United States

1. The Secretary of War has directed me to inform you that the President has appointed and commissioned you a temporary Second Lieutenant, Army of the United States, effective this date, in the grade shown in the address above. Your serial number is shown after A above.

2. This commission to continue in force during the pleasure of the President of the United States for the time being, and for the duration of the present emergency and six months thereafter unless sooner terminated.

3. There is inclosed herewith a form for oath of office which you are requested to execute and return. The execution and return of the required oath of office constitute an acceptance of your appointment. No other evidence of acceptance is required. This letter should be retained by you as evidence of your appointment.

W. R. Slaughter
W. R. SLAUGHTER,
Colonel, Ord. Dept.,
Commandant.

member. Interestingly, we had to list our first, second and third choices, and everyone in the class of I-62 who chose bomb disposal, first, second or third, was assigned to bomb disposal. I called Julie after I had made my choice, and I made my choice because I was very un-mechanical. Most of the men in my class had tinkered with cars and were mechanically inclined—I was not. So, I thought, choosing bomb disposal was a good move because I could start out with everyone else knowing nothing about it. As I say, I called Julie, and said, "Guess what I chose, dear" and she said, "Knowing you, you probably chose bomb disposal," and I said, "What else can we talk about on this phone call?"

She always wondered at my sanity in choosing one of the riskiest branches of the service possible. In fact, Ernie Pyle, the famous war correspondent, had said in one of his columns, "If your husband or your son goes in the ordnance department, you have nothing to worry about— he will be safe throughout the war. Unless he goes into one of two branches: tank recovery or bomb disposal." My mother was equally dismayed when she heard the one I had chosen.

"My son sent it to me a year ago, but I'm afraid to plug it in"

So we were now into six weeks of intensive training as potential bomb disposal officers. The saying at Aberdeen Proving Grounds was "you go up fast in bomb disposal." We practiced on various bombs, none of which were actually live. We learned about German fuzes, about American fuzes, about the ways of disposing bombs, ammunition, booby traps, how to approach them and what they could do to you.

Julie, who had left Newport News when I went into OCS, happily returned with our daughter, when I found a cabin in Sherwood Forest (a small community near Aberdeen) for the six weeks that I would be training to be a bomb disposal man. Marion, a visiting friend, taught Frances, now a little over one year, to say "I'm a Yankee by gum" which made quite a hit with our Southern neighbors.

ORDNANCE BOMB DISPOSAL CENTER
berdeen Proving Ground, Maryla

BOMB DISPOSAL OFFICERS' COURSE
12 June 1944 - 29 July 1944

Subcourse	Description	Student Hours
I.	ADMINISTRATION	9
II.	GENERAL SUBJECTS Introduction to course; history of Bomb Disposal; organization and operation of the Squad, Separate; military explosives.	18
III.	PRECAUTIONARY MEASURES Safety and evacuation; protective works; explosives handling, demolition precautions; safety in B. D. operations.	6
IV.	BOMB RECONNAISSANCE Flight and penetration of bombs; effects of exploding bombs; diagnosis of unexploded bombs; reporting and categories, field problems.	18
V.	ACCESS Methods of access; use of power tools and pumps; rigging and bomb handling.	25
VI.	BOMB IDENTIFICATION Characteristics and identification of bombs of enemy and allied rations.	50
VII.	FUZE IDENTIFICATION AND OPERATION A study of the fuzes used by enemy and allied countries for initiating bomb detonations as well as the more important artillery fuzes.	95
VIII.	MINES Identification; basic fuze operation and precautionary measures for all types of sea mines,	27
IX.	DISPOSAL OF UNEXPLODED BOMBS Demolition methods; neutralization methods, technique of handling unexploded bombs.	25
X.	BASIC MILITARY SUBJECTS Drill; knots and splices; booby traps; land mines; malaria control; censorship; utilization of manpower in the Army.	42
XI.	SUPERVISED ATHLETICS Calisthenics and organized games.	21
	TOTAL	336

One thing I never got used to was receiving a salute from midshipmen in Annapolis. They were two to four years into their quest for commissions and were saluting a second lieutenant who was commissioned in only twelve weeks.

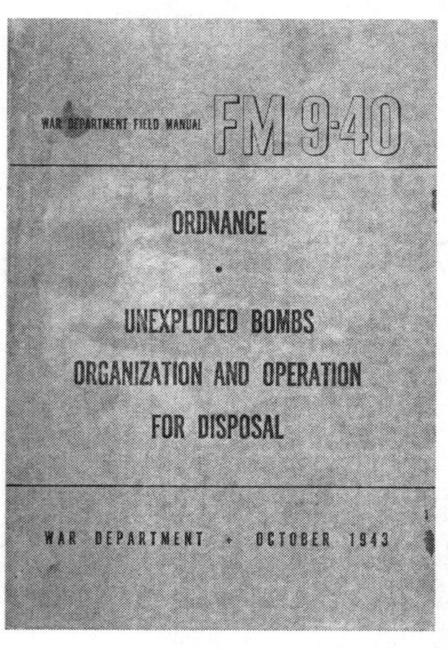

In six weeks they announced that we were ready to go out and risk our lives as bomb disposal officers. In October 1943, the war department issued FM 9-40, a 4" by 6", 148 page field manual titled, *Unexploded Bombs: Organization and Operation for Disposal.* In addition to describing the duties and responsibilities of bomb disposal units, it listed all that was known at the time of German, Italian, and Japanese bombs and projectiles. Presumably this was to be the "bible" for bomb disposal personnel. I was graduated from bomb disposal school on July 29th 1944, and first saw the manual in March of 2010 when my daughter found a copy for sale on the Internet. So much for my "bible." Maybe it was "Top Secret" and couldn't be shared with the troops defuzing and destroying these bombs.

Well and good. I attached the red "bomb" patch to my uniform, announcing my new profession to all who happened to look. I was transferred to Fort Jay on Governor's Island in New York Harbor, where we were possibly the only bomb disposal company then in existence, as squads had replaced companies in this work. Sometime back, the army had decided that the most effective way to handle bomb disposal was to have an officer and six non-commissioned officers, a squad of men, that would be sent wherever the explosives were found. But, on Fort Jay, we had a bomb disposal company (typically 75-200 men) whose sole responsibility was going over to Greenpoint, Brooklyn and watching as battlefield scrap was unloaded from barges. Big magnets dropped the scrap on the ground and we would go through it, looking to see if there were any explosives in there. This came about due to the army urging all field commanders overseas to send any battlefield scrap steel back to the U.S. to be sent to various mills to be melted down and made into whatever battle weapons were needed. There had been a few instances where some of the battlefield scrap turned out to have explosives still in it and a couple of blast furnaces were blown up as a result. So the government decided that all scrap had to be screened before it went off to the mills, and this was the function of the 1220th bomb disposal company. Every day in the hot sun, a bored group of enlisted men, with one or two officers supervising, would go over and examine all this battlefield scrap picking out the occasional explosive that had gotten by the field commanders.

ORDNANCE BOMB DISPOSAL CENTER
Aberdeen Proving Ground, Maryland

This is to certify that

Winfield Firman

2nd Lt.,Ord.Dept.

has successfully completed the Bomb Disposal Course prescribed for officers in the United States Army for the period of 12 June 1944 to 29 July 1944 and is declared proficient in all subjects included in the course as outlined on the reverse side of this sheet.

This certificate is issued pursuant to paragraph 16 (c), AR 350-110, September 1, 1942.

E. H. BENNETT
1st Lt., Ord. Dept.,
Adjutant

Eagle Staff photo

AIR BOMB DUG UP—Dropped from plane, this bomb had buried itself five feet in earth. Bomb disposal men dug it up, heard (through a stethoscope) time clock ticking, stopped the clock and are seen raising the bomb into a truck for disposal in "bomb cemetery." This was a simulated operation at foot of Dupont St. by men who carried out the real thing behind battle lines in Europe and Africa. Note heaped-up Italian poison gas shells.

Chapter Seven

MUSTARD GAS AND TRUE LOVE

Now we come to the infamous mustard gas bombs. Some enterprising officer in North Africa had come across almost 2,000 mustard gas bombs that the Italians had used in fighting Haile Selassie and his Ethiopian army, well before World War II. The officer steamed out the mustard gas, or so he thought, and then shipped these empty bomb casings back to Greenpoint, to ultimately go to steel mills. The problem was that it is almost impossible to get all of the mustard gas out of a bomb. It still smells horrible and sitting in the sun in Greenpoint, Brooklyn did not help. It was a terrible smell that sickened everybody that came close to it, so the army said, "I want you and the 1220th bomb disposal company to get rid of those bomb casings." We had three officers reporting to the colonel in the bomb disposal company, and we drew lots to see who would take these out to sea and dump them over the International Ledge. Lieutenant S. lost, and on a rainy Sunday morning, the bomb casings were loaded onto a sea-going tug, and with the lieutenant and a couple of men from the bomb disposal company aboard, they headed out to sea to get rid of these mustard gas bombs once and for all. It was a miserable day, cold and rainy, and that tug was up and down and up and down and they were all getting sick, aided I'm sure by the smell of the mustard gas bombs. So they said, "Why do we go all the way out to the continental shelf, why don't we dump the bombs now? We'll never see them again." They all quickly agreed, and over went the bombs, and that was to be the last of them. They came back to our unit on Fort Jay, and said the mission was accomplished, and that was that.

Now we go a couple of weeks into the future, and Win Firman is the Officer of the Day which, in army parlance, means the officer that has duty at night. So I was to take my turn sitting at the desk, or lying in my bunk, and I was responsible for anything that happened in the world of explosives that particular night. Well, nothing had ever happened. And it seemed to me that nothing was ever going to happen, so I called Julie, who was living with her parents in Scarsdale, New York and I said, "Julie, come on into Fort Jay and you and I will spend the night at the officer's club because I'm on duty, and I can't stay in my bunk" and so forth and Julie said "Wonderful!" and she came in and met me. I said to the sergeant, who was the non-commissioned duty officer for the night, "If anything happens, call me at the officers' club, and I will immediately come over." So Julie and I went off happily to have a night together.

As I said, nothing had ever happened at night to warrant a call to the 1220th bomb disposal company, but on **this** night, which I chose to spend with my wife, dozens of those damn mustard gas bombs washed up on the shore at Greenwich, Connecticut. Immediately the police called the bomb disposal company. The sergeant on duty called the officers' club to notify me, and was told, "We do not disturb any guests at night."

So all through the night, while the police in Greenwich worried about the bombs, I slept happily. The next day, it hit the fan. The commanding general at Fort Jay had me on the carpet to explain why I wasn't on duty as a I was supposed to be as Officer of the Day. Well, I somehow escaped that one—but just barely. And I never took my role as Officer of the Day for granted, after that event.

Chapter Eight

THAT OLD BROKEN NOSE

I had broken my nose twice in three years of football at Amherst College well before face guards were added to the helmets. (Yes, I also broke my ankle playing softball! What can I say?) Then, in basic training at Fort Eustis, I was running down the line of 40 mm anti-aircraft guns to get some tools, when someone called to me and I looked back. As I did this, I swerved and turned my head, and I ran smack into a gun barrel at head height. The result? My third broken nose.

Julie, who with daughter Frances, was then living with me in Newport News, came to the Fort Eustis Hospital and broke out laughing. "What is so funny?" I asked. Said my good wife, "With your black eyes and swollen nose you look just like Peter Lorre!" So much for sympathy.

The surgeon who rebuilt my nose, later, at the Fort Jay Hospital gave me a local anesthetic—thus, I could hear all the crunching of the bones as he cut into the deviated septum. When "the doc" had finished he surveyed his work proudly and said, "Lieutenant, if I had not run out of bone ('mine') I could have given you a Roman nose. Too bad it will always remain a pug." I like the pug nose just fine. Still have it in fact, and have, thankfully, not broken it ever again.

Firman, number 35, on his way to his first broken nose

The infamous pre-wedding broken ankle

Chapter Nine

THE BIG STORY

But there were more dramatic events going on at this time. And though I was on the sidelines, they had a large impact on all of us, especially those of us at Fort Jay and the good citizens of New England, where this particular drama unfolded.

Two German spies were tried by a military tribunal at Fort Jay and, on Valentine's Day in February of 1945 were found guilty of violating the eighty-second article of war, which makes the death penalty mandatory for any person who, in the time of the war, shall be found lurking or acting as a spy.

William Colepaugh, an American defector, and German agent Erich Gimpal, had come ashore in Maine from a U-boat on November 29th. Starting out in a snowstorm, the spies made their way to New York City. Later, Colepaugh confessed his status to a friend and, in late December, the F.B.I. arrested the pair who were imprisoned and tried at Fort Jay, found guilty, and sentenced to die by hanging.

Through a friendly officer who attended the trial, I learned of the guilty verdict even before the New York newspapers did. I published the news in the 1220th bomb disposal company's mimeographed newspaper, "The Fuze," almost as soon as the New York Times, the Herald Tribune, and The New York Daily News did. A small claim to fame.

Newspaper headlines read "Two Spies to Die by Hanging." The

military commission that consisted of seven officers of the Second Service Command announced the findings. The President of the Commission was quoted as saying "Erich Gimpel, this commission, by a secret written ballot, finds you guilty upon all three counts, and you are hereby sentenced to be hanged by the neck until dead." Colepaugh received the same sentence. It was said that neither man flinched or faltered as they walked from the room under custody of guards.

Oddly, both spies escaped execution—first because of a moratorium caused by President Roosevelt's death and secondly, when new president, Harry S. Truman commuted their sentences to life imprisonment. The American traitor, Colepaugh, was paroled after 15 years and lived in the U.S. until his death in 2005 at age 86. Gimpel was paroled after serving 10 years in prison, deported to Brazil and also died at age 86 in 1996.

Chapter Ten

NEARLY A SPY MYSELF

We were all supposed to be very happy to be in safe berths stateside but I felt that the war was passing me by and I was extremely eager to get on with whatever I was going to do. As bomb disposal had a very high priority, the only unit to which one of us could transfer was infantry. So, much to the colonel's distress, I requested a transfer to the infantry. And he was going to veto it, because he felt it was extremely disloyal. Several days later I was called to Whitehall Street and when I showed up there somebody in civilian clothes interrogated me, looked at my identification, and then sent me in. I found out later that he was a non-commissioned officer in the O.S.S. (Office of Strategic Services), which was the predecessor of the C.I.A. The officer interviewing me there had said he had noted that I was unhappy at Fort Jay and he had a proposition for me. Those guys knew everything about me. The proposition was to train me someplace in the Southwest for a few weeks and then to drop me behind enemy lines in the Pacific on one of the islands. Either drop me by plane or put me in by submarine and I would go in to be an island watcher—shades of "South Pacific"—where I would be doing hazardous duty behind Japanese lines. The O.S.S. officer told me that it was not really very hazardous, that they took very good care of their people. So I said, "Yes. To get out of Fort Jay and Greenpoint, Brooklyn, I would be happy to take on this assignment for the O.S.S."

He was very pleased and we shook hands on it. When I told Julie, she thought I was crazy—AGAIN. But fate intervened. A week or so later, the order came out for all stateside units, including the Second Army, the Eastern Defense Command, and every unit in the United States to free up 10% of their officers and enlisted men for overseas duty. Well, the colonel could not have been happier. He knew who was going to be the officer he chose to go overseas and it was Win Firman, obviously. So, quickly, I was transferred to Aberdeen Proving Grounds, for the big move overseas. I'm sure that to this day, the O.S.S./C.I.A. wonders where that cowardly Lieutenant Firman disappeared to, rather than carry out his assignment behind enemy lines. They're probably still looking for me.

CONFIDENTIAL

Copy

OFFICE OF STRATEGIC SERVICES
ROOM 107, North Building
WASHINGTON, D. C.

SHP:jah
14 February 1945

SUBJECT: Firman, Winfield, Lt. 01558456

TO : Commanding Officer, 1220th SCU, Ft Jay, Governors Island, New York

THRU: Commanding General, Second Service Command, Governors Island 4, New York

1. Subject officer is reported to possess certain qualifications that may fit him for duty with the Office of Strategic Services.

2. If qualified, the nature of such duty will be of unusual importance, and will require:

a. Good physical condition.
b. XXXXXXXXXXXXXXXXXXXXXXX
c. XXXXXXXXXXXXXXXXXXXXXXXXXX

3. If convenient to the subject's commanding officer to do so, a brief summary as to the subject's general fitness, trustworthiness, capacity, and abilities appended to the Forms 2205 would be appreciated by this service.

4. If and when transfer is to be accomplished, request will be made through channels.

5. Subject will not be informed that he is under consideration by the Office of Strategic Services.

6. In the event subject officer has been transferred from your command, it is requested that communication be forwarded by indorsement to proper station.

For the Director:

Stamped/ S. H. Parkins
S. H. PARKINS
Major, AUS
Personnel Procurement Branch

2 Incls.
Forms 2205.

10 March 1945

201-Firman, Winfield, Lt. 01558456

Recommendation

Commanding General, Second Service Command, ASF,
Governors Island, New York 4, N.Y.

ATTN: Director, Miliery Personnel Division
50 Broadway, New York 4, N. Y.

1. As recommended in paragraph 3, letter dated 14 February 1945, from Personnel Procurement Branch, the following is submitted:

Lt. Winfield Firman is a resourceful, quiet, well-poised, and enthusiastic young officer - rates high on leadership; displays aggressiveness, a willingness to work and inspires confidence in his men.

E. L. SHERWOOD
Lt.Colonel, OD
Commanding

Reluctant recommendation from Colonel Sherwood

SIXTH ARMY'S KRUEGER

Chapter Eleven

INTO THE REAL WAR

So, now we begin a new era. At Aberdeen Proving Grounds, we wondered whether we were going to Europe or to the Pacific. We had some intimation that it was going to be the Pacific when we were issued suntans ("summer" uniforms) and mosquito netting, while it was winter in Europe. Sure enough, that was our destination. A fast trip across the country by train and then flying over to Manila in a large commercial aircraft. I was chosen as the messenger officer and had all the top secret dispatches in a locked briefcase chained to my wrist. When we arrived at Pearl Harbor for refueling, I was not allowed to disembark from the plane, and only saw it as some lights through a small window that night. A highlight of the trip was that as we flew towards Manila, the pilot of our plane saw a freighter in the water below us and decided to fly down to see if it was U.S. or Japanese. I always thought that was a foolish move. If it had been a Japanese freighter—one with anti-aircraft guns—we'd have been a big, fat, sitting duck. But it turned out to be a U.S. freighter and all was well as we continued on to Manila. There I sat it out for a week or so in a *repple depple*, which is short for replacement depot. The only interesting thing that happened to us there, besides being constantly importuned by 12 and 14 year-old prostitutes, was that one night a large group of us were watching a stateside movie when the projector broke. They turned on the floodlights and there were three Japanese soldiers, sitting there, enjoying the movie. They made a quick exit when the lights went on. We always thought it was rather amusing that they were sitting there and there weren't even Japanese subtitles for the movie.

Shortly thereafter I was assigned to the 106th bomb disposal squad. And quickly found my first live bomb. Unfortunately, it was under the headquarters of General Krueger in San Fernando, 45 miles above Manila. General Krueger was head of the Sixth Army and little did I know who I was dealing with on my very first bomb. Turns out General Krueger was one of the big guns of the war. After I examined the bomb, I decided it was really too badly damaged to try to take it out of there. The manual says that the bomb disposal officer decides when a bomb is too badly damaged to be removed, and may elect to have it blown up in situ, after sandbagging it. General Krueger's chief of staff, a full colonel, said to me, "Lieutenant, you may think that the bomb looks badly damaged and you may decide that you want to blow it up where it is but I will tell you this: If you try to take the bomb out from under General Krueger's headquarters and it blows up, you'll still be better off than telling General Krueger you're going to blow up a bomb under his headquarters." Well, that was a dilemma. I decided after looking at it again, that maybe it wasn't as badly damaged as I had thought the first time. Probably, any damaged bomb, being my first bomb, would've looked too badly damaged to me. So, I went in with a pipe wrench, took the fuze out, and we took the 250 pound general purpose bomb from under the HQ and took it away. My first bomb was behind me.

Chapter Twelve

AND LIFE WENT ON AT HOME

In the summer of 1945 the wives of the four Firman boys were all expecting and the Firman boys themselves were all at war. Even in the midst of the world at war, we were, after all, family and we still stayed connected and had as much fun as we could. In this case, we started a pool on the sex of each still-to-be-born child and the order in which they would be born. Surprisingly, eight of the forty-six entrants guessed right on the sex of the four and the order of birth. Nearly 18% shared the proceeds.

July 9, 1945, I received a telegram from the "Colonel", as I called him, Julie's father. When we were married I was stumped as to what to call Julie's father. Her mother, Sarah Fisher was easy, I called her *Sally* as did all the kids and grandkids in future years. But here was a rather stern senior partner in a major law firm, so *dad* or *pop* was unthinkable and I could not see

Sgt. William & Capt. Royal Firman

Joe Firman in North Africa

calling him by his first name, Marion, and saying *Mr. Fisher* for the next fifty years seemed a little unfriendly. A dilemma for the new son-in-law. A sudden thought occurred. He had been a colonel in the National Guard after serving as a captain in France during World War I. *Colonel* had a nice ring and he liked it. So, *Colonel* it was. His other kids liked it as well and after a while even his wife, Sally, began calling him that. To the day he died his family called him *Colonel.* What a happy thought, thought I.

The telegram he sent, had been sent June 29th to announce the arrival of my son, Tom. The telegram had gone to San Francisco and had been air-mailed from there. So, by the time I got the long-awaited news, Thomas Randolph Firman was 10 days old. A cartoon in *Yank Magazine* showed a G.I. running to his buddies with a telegram in his hand and yelling, "Hooray, my wife just had a bouncing 12 points toward my discharge!"

THE GREAT FIRMAN BABY SEX POOL
(Promoted by Lt. Winfield Firman)

Thomas Randolph Firman
Scarsdale, New York
June 29, 1945

John VanEss Firman
White Plains, New York
August 28, 1945

Cynthia Pamela Firman
Cleveland, Ohio
August 7, 1945

Melanie Anne Firman
Wimbledon, England
September 26, 1945

THE WINNAHS! THE WINNAHS! THE WINNAHS!

Lt. Bryan Bell, Jr.
Margery D. Cross
Sgt. William W. Firman
Eleanor Alley

Winifred E. Vose
S.G. Willcox
Helen F. Sweet
Lt. Winfield Firman

PLACED:

Barbara Alley
Janet Cross Keyes
Marion Fisher

ALSO RAN:

*Carol Butler
Catharine K. Firman
Donald S. Hutton
Sgt. Joseph H. Firman
Miller Cross
Ray H. Haun
*George M. Humphrey
Harold I. Cross
*Pamela Firman
Capt. Royal Firman, Jr.
Lillian H. Cross
Frances Hessey
Evans Hessey
Sarah R. Fisher
Phyllis K. Willcox
*Pamela Humphrey
T.L. Brantley
Lt. Comdr. Royal Firman
Alexander W. Alley
Juliet Firman
Anne B. Beckway
Lucille Braucher
Lt. Floyd G. Arpan
Helen L. Brantley
SK/2c Paul J. Keyes
William W. Steffey
Dr. Fred Flynn
Daphne Firman
Mildred Haun
Eleanor Arpan
Eleanor Flynn
Eleanor Miller
Fank Braucher
Evans Vose

*Holiday Hill Farm entry

50¢ ticket pays $3.00 – No place or show money

N.B. Bookmaker made no profit. He had to contribute 50¢ to make the tote come out even.

MILLER CROSS, BOOKMAKER

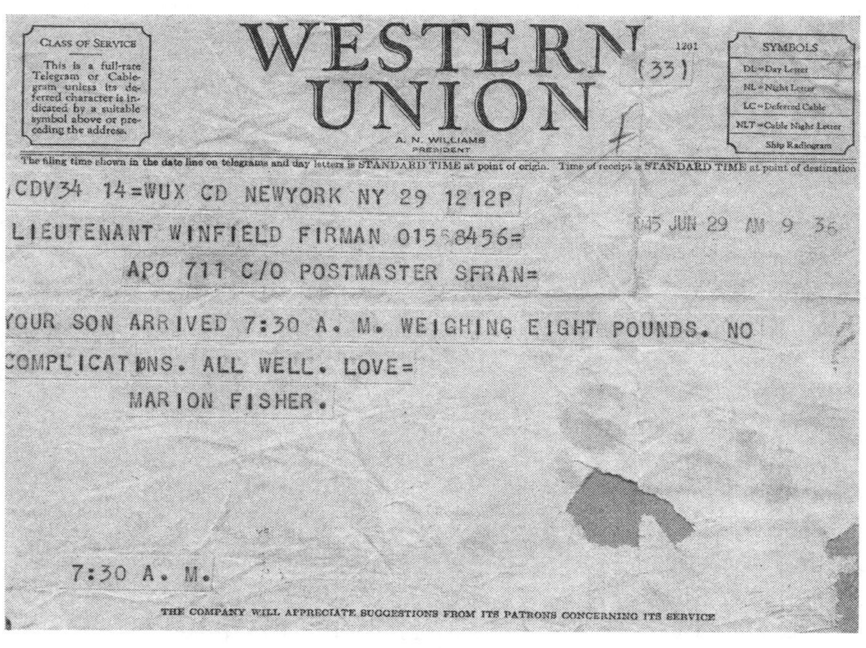

CLASS OF SERVICE
This is a full-rate Telegram or Cablegram unless its deferred character is indicated by a suitable symbol above or preceding the address.

WESTERN UNION

A. N. WILLIAMS
PRESIDENT

1201

(33)

SYMBOLS
DL=Day Letter
NL=Night Letter
LC=Deferred Cable
NLT=Cable Night Letter
Ship Radiogram

The filing time shown in the date line on telegrams and day letters is STANDARD TIME at point of origin. Time of receipt is STANDARD TIME at point of destination

CDV34 14=WUX CD NEWYORK NY 29 1212P

LIEUTENANT WINFIELD FIRMAN 015[illegible]8456=

APO 711 C/O POSTMASTER SFRAN=

1945 JUN 29 AM 9 36

YOUR SON ARRIVED 7:30 A. M. WEIGHING EIGHT POUNDS. NO COMPLICATIONS. ALL WELL. LOVE=

MARION FISHER.

7:30 A. M.

THE COMPANY WILL APPRECIATE SUGGESTIONS FROM ITS PATRONS CONCERNING ITS SERVICE

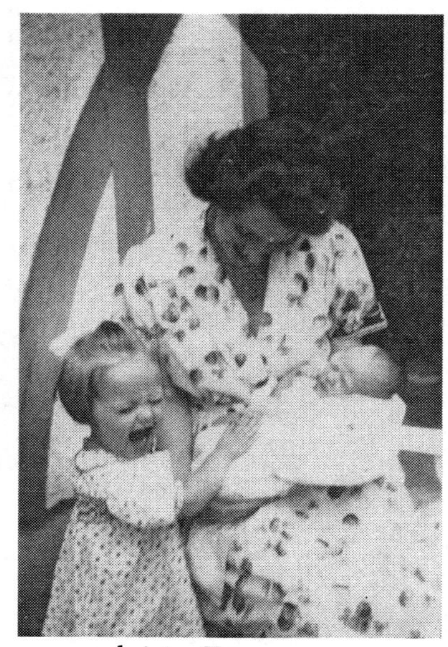

The new arrival Thomas with mom and sister Frances

Chapter Thirteen

LIFE AT WAR

Now, we were set to work to pick up the bombs that G-2, the intelligence division, found all over Manila and San Fernando. I was using some top-secret equipment that had been given to me at Aberdeen Proving Grounds. One was a spring-loaded wrench, which I fastened to the bomb fuze, got 50 yards away and pulled the cord; the wrench would pull on the fuze, turning it and falling back when I released it, and if I did this two or three times, the fuze would drop out of the bomb, thereby sparing me from being right at the bomb if anything went wrong. Another piece of equipment was a piston, perhaps 18 inches long, into the tail of which was put a crimped 50 caliber cartridge. The other end had a steel slug which was placed up against the bomb fuze. A blasting cap, with a black powder safety fuse, was set off and the piston would drive that steel slug right through the fuze. My squad and I would be 100-200 yards away when it happened.

But each of these procedures, designed for the safety of the bomb disposal squad, took a minimum of half an hour. Particularly difficult was finding the steel slug that had shaved off the fuze. As each morning, G-2 would present us with a list of 40-50 locations where live explosives had been found, one half hour per explosive was a luxury we didn't have. After several attempts to use this equipment and finding no way to speed up the procedures, we returned the equipment to the Ordnance Department and went back to our trusty pipe wrench as our principal tool.

After a few weeks, I was transferred to the 208th bomb disposal squad in Batangas, 60 miles south of Manila. It was a unit that had been overseas for a period of time; they were well-organized and well-disciplined, and their previous commanding officer had been a Captain Reid who was most beloved by the six non-commissioned officers of the 208th. It was fascinating to read their letters to home. All letters from enlisted men had to be reviewed, edited, and censored by an officer to make sure they were not giving away critical information that, if intercepted, would be of use to the enemy. As one cartoon in Yank Magazine had it, an officer was saying to an enlisted man, holding his letter, "Yes, you know it's Thursday, and I know it's Thursday, but do the Japanese know it's Thursday?" In writing these letters, they would say, "Oh, we sure miss Captain Reid, he was a wonderful man, so great, it was sad to see him get enough points and go home." Then often remembering that I would be reading the letters, they would put in something such as, "but Lieutenant Firman seems like a nice enough guy." I often came second in that particular operation, so, I began the routine of taking my squad out everyday to visit the many places in which G-2 had found explosives.

In Batangas, our squad was offered the services of a Japanese P.O.W. to clean our tents, polish our boots, and help with the chores of bomb disposal. Kazuhalu was delighted to leave the P.O.W. camp each day and he couldn't have been more helpful. His request said, "Please sighn tipe writing name card. Should every day to see you. My name Kazuhalu Nissi." He did wash a cork-lined Japanese sword scabbard I had. From then on, the sword would rust when put in the scabbard.

Unfortunately, so many daily stops to pick up explosives made it seem like a milk run and we had to guard against carelessness—our greatest danger.

The Filipinos would steam out artillery shells and bombs and use the TNT or picric acid for fishing. Once they got their hands on safety fuse and blasting caps, they would put them together, insert them in a ¼ pound TNT, light the fuse, and toss it into the water. The fish would come around the bubbles and KABOOM. There would be 15 or 20 dead fish there. So, if you had wanted to traffic in blasting caps or safety fuse, you could have gotten many things from the Filipinos: grass skirts, blouses, whatever. Also, they had a bad habit of taking the artillery shells from which they had steamed the TNT and using them as a fireplaces in their small homes. This, of course, had unfortunate consequences whenever they had left in some of the TNT. Lighting a fire in the fireplace tended to set off the artillery shell. So, when the authorities cracked down on this practice, wherever we went we would collect hundreds and hundreds of artillery shells that had been picked up by the Filipinos.

Sgt. St. Marie, Firman & Cpl. Robinson

Dig 'em out, defuze 'em, truck 'em away!

Chapter Fourteen

THE BIG BOMB

One interesting excursion was the result of being directed by G-2 to a 2,000 pound bomb that been dropped and failed to go off. My squad went out there, stopping en route to have a lunch of one of our "ten-in-one" rations, which were excellent. These rations were designed to feed ten people one meal, but it was too much for our seven-man squad, so we always shared it with Filipino children. Arriving at the bomb, we were impressed. It was huge! Half again as tall as a man and containing 2,000 pounds of TNT. There was not much we could do as far as moving it. All we had was a jeep and a 2 ½ ton truck (called a 6' x 6' or deuce and a half) so we had to leave the removal of the bomb to the engineers who could bring in heavy equipment, perhaps a crane and winches, and hoist it out of there. But I did intend to take the fuze from the nose of the bomb and render it inert. I put the pipe wrench on the fuze, and was starting to twist it when I glanced up and to my amusement noticed that all of the onlookers, scores of Filipino residents, had their fingers in their ears so if the bomb went off they wouldn't hear it. Of course, if it had gone off, it would have killed everybody within half a mile, so it was useless to be holding your ears so that the sound of a 2,000 pound bomb going off would not injure your eardrums. This was a U.S. bomb, and it presented no problem to us. We took out the fuze and we notified the engineers, and if it was still sitting there enterprising

Filipinos would take off the metal sheath and begin to chip away at the TNT for fishing purposes. Later we had to deal with three more of these one-ton babies after a motor vehicle accident.

One other incident that was of interest was when we were awakened in the middle of the night by the military police who said that there was a bomb in the main road from Batangas to Manila. The traffic had been stopped in both directions. Would we come over and get rid of the bomb? So we dressed and jumped into our jeep and truck and drove over and, sure enough, there was a 175 kg Japanese bomb. The Japanese had dug a deep hole in the road, put the bomb in tail end first, and then covered it over with dirt and a little macadam figuring that in due course, U.S. traffic would uncover the bomb and blow up a vehicle or two. The Japanese had made one small mistake: they had not taken off the arming wire to the fuze, which was designed to prevent it from going off prematurely. So the primer was permanently separated from the striker and the fuze was never going to go off, and the bomb was never going to blow up.

So, with hundreds of excited onlookers, we used our old familiar pipe wrench to take the fuze out, and then hauled the bomb out and dumped it in the back of our truck as if it were a chunk of rock.

170 pound man & 2000 pound bomb

Chapter Fifteen

BOY SCOUTS AND SOLDIERS

I had heard that the Scoutmaster of Troop 3 in Scarsdale, Major Kevney O'Connor, was in the army and in Manila. I had been in Troop 3 from Tenderfoot to Eagle Scout and I was the Junior Assistant Scoutmaster before I went off to college. I had always been close to "the Major" as we called him and looked forward to seeing him again after some six years.

Kevney O'Connor

The Major was a remarkable man. As a major in World War I, he was released from active service after losing a lung in a German gas attack (which did not keep him from being a chain smoker). He stayed on in The Reserve and, when I finally caught up with him, he had nine fogies (hitches) and was drawing 45% additional base pay.

He had run Troop 3 like a military unit—whistle meant stop still or lose the five "discipline" points for your patrol, trooping of the colors, formal retreat and taps with the lights out at the end of scout meeting. The Major believed in close order drill and practice we did—in the Scout House in fall and winter and on the high school football field in the spring.

The Major led the troop in drill competition of all Scarsdale scout troops each Memorial Day (with West Point officers judging) and won the competition year after year. In 1936, Major O'Connor presented his six patrol leaders, his two senior patrol leaders, and his Junior Assistant Scoutmaster (the author) to the judges and asked them to pick one to drill Troop 3's sixty scouts in the competition. They declined his offer so the Major selected me and we won again. Yawn.

When the U.S. went to war, the Major was chosen to head the Selective Service Board and couldn't wait to get his former scouts into the armed forces. When I finally tracked him down in Manila, I was surprised to find he was a captain in the Military Police—a position he chose for his second war rather than accept the rank of major in the Ordnance Department where he would serve stateside. When we finally met, the "Major" (now a captain) had been overseas since the spring of '43 (Australia, New Guinea, the Philippines) and now had 122 points (N.B. see subsequent discussion of points necessary for discharge and how they were earned), far more than necessary to return to the U.S. but he was hoping to be in the invasion of Japan.

We were tickled to see each other, although I had difficulty calling him Captain after years of thinking of him as MAJOR O'Connor. We had a long bull session followed by lunch. He asked after Julie and our two young ones, and remembered brother Bill who had been in the troop a year or two. He told me 13 former members of the troop had been killed in the war, a number of them who I knew well. Rather staggering number from one Boy Scout troop. The major was remembered by all former members of Troop 3 because part of their marching song went:

With leaders like our Fred
And the Major at our head
At any goal undaunted we
as scouts and men we'll always be
the best troop you will ever see
We are Scarsdale's own Troop 3

In parting, Major/Captain O'Connor said, "I always knew you were made to order for the army."

Chapter Sixteen

CLOSE CALLS

As you would expect, we had several close calls in defuzing bombs and blowing up artillery shells. It was quite natural that sooner or later, something would go wrong. One time, we had put a pile of bombs together in the middle of nowhere to blow them up. We had put a blasting cap into one of the bombs and a piece of safety fuse into the cap. We lit it and took off in our jeep. We always had two choices: running an electric wire to the fuze, prohibiting us from getting very far away because we had a wire connection to our detonator which set it off. We seldom could get more than 50 or 75 yards away from the explosion. The advantage was that you could look all around to make sure that nobody was in the vicinity before the cry went out "Fire in the hole" and someone twisted the "hellbox" or detonator and up would go the explosives. Obviously, the advantage of using a safety fuse was that we could get miles away from the explosion before it occurred and, just as obviously, the big disadvantage was that we had no way of knowing who might wander into the area after we had taken off leaving the fuse burning.

In this particular case, we had felt that the bomb was far enough away from homes and people so that we were safe in using the safety fuse. After the explosion, the squad's sergeant and I walked back to see if all the bombs had exploded. A parafrag bomb had broken open and was burning when we got to it. So we turned and started to run and we had gotten about ten steps away when it went off. But basically, they are designed to throw an umbrella of shrapnel, which is where the term comes from, "parachute-fragmentation bomb." Dropped by parachute, it fragments and covers a large area with the steel pieces of the bomb. We were still within the umbrella of that spread of shrapnel so it went harmlessly over our heads. If we had been able to run further, we might not have been so fortunate.

On one other occasion when we were blowing up a number of artillery shells, we were within reach of Filipino houses, and therefore decided we couldn't use the safety fuse. We made an electrical connection so that we could make sure there was nobody in the area when the cry of "Fire in the hole" went out. We hid behind a few tiny trees, which were very little protection, and fired off the charge that blew up the bombs and the artillery shells. We could hear the pieces of the shells flying by us as we scrunched down behind the trees. After it was over and we were on our way back to our vehicles, a Filipino man came to us smiling broadly and showed us a four or five pound chunk of artillery shell that had fallen through the thatched roof of his house. We were dumbfounded because, had that killed anyone, we would have spent a lot of time, perhaps with a court-martial, explaining why this had happened. He regarded it as somewhat of a joke, but we were pretty well shaken over that particular incident.

Another assignment we had was when we were asked to find a way to destroy three Japanese ammunition barges that the U.S. Air Force had sunk in Batangas Bay earlier in the war. These barges were perhaps 20 feet deep, but presented somewhat of a problem for navigation, and so we were asked by the Navy to destroy these barges. I, of course, asked where the Navy Bomb Disposal was, but there was no unit within 500 miles, so it fell to us. They assigned us a boat and I took my squad to the torpedo boat one morning, with our satchels full of explosives, and out we went. Was it a torpedo boat? 65 years later I don't remember. In one report I mention a cutter, which suggests a larger boat. The skipper asked if we had ever seen an "ash can" explode ("ash can" being a term for a depth charge). We said no, we never had, so he fired one from the rear deck of the boat and it made a very satisfying underwater explosion. We asked how he was going to explain this, because those things must have cost a couple of thousand dollars, and he said, "Oh, I'll just say we thought we heard a submarine and fired it as a precaution."

We arrived at the scene of the ammunition barges, got into our swimsuits, and dove down. Looking at them, the project did not seem to be that difficult, though we were working in 15-20 feet of water. So while one of the squad held the safety fuse above the water, I dove down to the first ammunition barge and attached a satchel charge to a bomb. The safety fuse went into the blasting cap and the blasting cap into the TNT in the satchel charge. I came back to the surface, lit the fuse, and those of us in the water (two or three of us) were picked up by the torpedo boat and were half a mile away when the explosion occurred. It destroyed the ammunition barge completely and, incidentally, brought a large group of Filipinos to the area because of the number of fish that had been killed. We repeated the process with barge two without incident, got away safely on the boat and had another very satisfying explosion. With barge number three, once I had positioned the satchel charge against several large bombs on the ammunition barge and had come to the surface, I lit the fuse. I missed the rope trailing from the PT boat as it went by. But the others in my squad were safely aboard and I was watching the boat disappear over the horizon while I was treading water over 70 or 80 thousand pounds of Japanese bombs that were set to go off. They came back for me and picked me up and I had really overreacted, because, as I think I said, safety fuse burns at about 45 seconds a foot. With twenty feet of fuse going down to the bomb, I had about 15 minutes to be picked up. It was a very scary sensation at the time. This incident is one of those mentioned in my citation for a bronze star later.

We continued to see the Navy men after our work with them. The skipper of the PT boat was squiring a woman from the Red Cross and he took her on seagoing trips, went to dances at the Red Cross (using our jeep) and when they were an "item" they discussed marriage—she with more interest than he. On one occasion she said to him "Wouldn't it be nice if we had a daughter and she, on growing up, married Win?" The skipper disillusioned her by pointing out that I was already married and had two children. Did I really look that young?

Addendum: When our Red Cross friend was returned to the states, the skipper and I received announcements of her wedding within a month. So much for overseas romances!

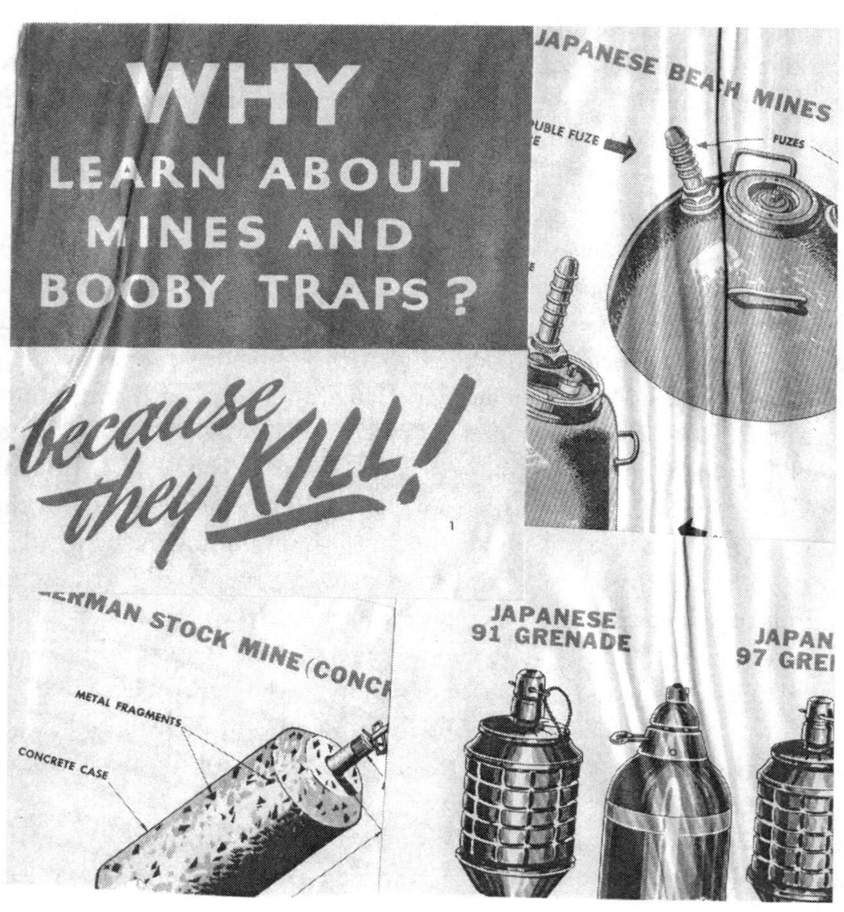
WHY
LEARN ABOUT
MINES AND
BOOBY TRAPS?
because they KILL!
JAPANESE BEACH MINES
UBLE FUZE
FUZES
ERMAN STOCK MINE (CONC
METAL FRAGMENTS
CONCRETE CASE
JAPANESE
91 GRENADE
JAPAN
97 GRE

Chapter Seventeen

A WEDDING

The young Filipino woman who did our laundry, whose sister was getting married, asked if we would take the bridal party to and from the Cathedral in our truck. Our entire squad was invited to the breakfast before the service, the church service, and the reception after. We accepted the invitation and agreed to the request.

Unfortunately for us, at that time a Catholic wedding service had to be performed in the church before sun-up. So at 5:00 am, Robbie, St. Marie and I took the jeep and truck to the bride's house and everybody sat down to a big breakfast that consisted of a great many dishes foreign and unappetizing to my taste. Afterwards, we took the whole wedding party to the big Cathedral in town with the siren sounding at their request. There were seven couples being married, so we sat through half of one high mass and all of another while our couple was getting married. Robbie thought it was very impressive but none of us could hear the priest and the entire ceremony was a bit lost to me. And, oddly, the bride and groom took no part in the wedding ceremony at all, except the communion, which everyone in the Cathedral who so wished took. I wouldn't have felt I was married, but they were and happy about it as all could see. We then took them all back with the bride and groom stopping at the photographers for picture-taking. Then, as the post-wedding party got under way, we three took off to get in reports, etc., promising to return. At about 10:00 we did and they immediately took us inside and began pouring us water glasses FULL of American whiskey. The squad killed a fifth of whiskey in about 20 minutes and then we started on the "Black Label"[2] whiskey and fried chicken, rice, and oranges. Quite a combination. Two fellows played a guitar and a ukulele and we all sang. Then we went out where a six-piece band was getting in some hot licks. I sang a couple of numbers with them and then as St. Marie was dancing with the singer of the band and Robbie was busily leading them, I realized that my number was up—I broke out in a tremendous sweat so I took off to the jeep and went to sleep there.

When the party was breaking up and the men came to the jeep, they woke me and I was promptly sick. We all drove back to the area with me more or less sober by then, Robbie absolutely polluted, and St. Marie in between. I went right to my cot to sleep so when I woke up for the Company Commander's meeting at 3:30, I felt pretty well. But while I slept, Robbie took off in the jeep before the others could stop him yelling, "Aureen, I want Aureen, where's Aureen!" (she was one of the bridesmaids). Biehl and St. Marie went after him in the truck and, after some real slapstick at the bride's house, they got him to come back when two of the women agreed to come with him. So they put him to bed and took off his shirt, trousers, and shoes and St. Marie took the girls back in the jeep. When he came back down the road there was Robbie in just his shorts running down the road waving a trip ticket. He had jumped in the truck and taken it across the ball diamond and then abandoned it.

What a day! By the time I got up, it was all quiet and last night, all we could do was laugh about it. It was certainly funny. Gee, Robbie was a panic—but I suppose we all were. In the morning only St. Marie had a hangover. That is about enough of a Filipino wedding for me—I couldn't survive another.

2. The "Black Label" whiskey was home made and called locally – and rightfully so - "White Lightning."

Chapter Eighteen

FAMILY IN WAR

Cmdr. Royal Firman

My father had gone from War Production Board into Military Government, attended school in Washington and was sent out to Okinawa as second-in-command of the military government there. Okinawa is perhaps 850 miles from Manila, and I thought it would be a lot of fun if I could get up there and drop in on the old man, perhaps surprise him. I hadn't seen him since he came down to pin my bars on when I was made a second lieutenant at Aberdeen Proving Grounds. We had corresponded some but had really been out of touch. It was interesting to his family, that with four sons in the service, all of them in the army, that he chose to go to the Navy. Probably part of his competitive spirit that Pop can do better than the boys who were sprinkled across the European theatre, from Joe with the infantry in North Africa to Bill in London with the OSS and Royal with the Air Force, also in London. I, of course, was in the Philippines.

So I went to the commanding officer of the larger unit, to which the bomb disposal squad is attached for rations and quarters, and told him of my plan to bum a ride to Okinawa to see the old man. He thought that was a great idea so he wrote on the back of a used envelope, "Lieutenant Firman has my permission to be away from his unit for a few days." Things were a little slow at the time in the bomb disposal arena, so it was agreed that I would fly up there, spend a few days, and then come back. This was August 14, 1945, and I had one of my squad members drive me to Manila where I could hitch a ride on a troop carrier plane going to Okinawa.

I finally found one going to Okinawa and was able to bum a ride on it, arriving in Okinawa someplace. I worked my way across the lines because the Japanese were still very active in that area and prepared to drop in on my father in the Military Government Headquarters on Okinawa. These headquarters were trim Quonset huts surrounded by grass and flowers and looking very, very Naval in their smartness. When I found his hut, I walked in and walked up to his desk where he was hard at work and I said, "Don't get up commander, this is an informal visit!" Understand that he hadn't seen me in a considerable period of time. I was now bright yellow from taking atabrine regularly (which was a preventative for malaria), I had a bushy mustache which he had never seen, and I was in rather grubby suntans with combat boots and a .45 at my hip. I was wearing a non-regulation hat that our laundress had made for me. So here was this disreputable looking lieutenant in front of a full commander in the Navy saying, "Don't get up." He looked up, didn't recognize me, and decided that probably this was some lunatic. I think I saw some smoke coming out of his ears. His face did get red, and as he was about to call the Shore Patrol to take this nut away he said, "Is that you Win?" Then he was up from his desk as we hugged each other, smiling ear to ear.

We spent the next two days enjoying our mini-reunion and having a great time. We took money from his fellow naval officers at bridge, we took money from them at poker, and when it came time to go, I was prepared to take half my winnings, except it was all in Okinawa script, which wouldn't have done me any good in the Philippines. So dad got all the takings, and we laughed about this a number of times in the ensuing years.

One interesting thing was when I was going up to the can at night, dad said, "Be sure to take your .45 with you," and I said, "Why, isn't the perimeter safe against Japanese?" and he said, "Yes it is but we have a very deadly snake, the fer-de-lance, which you might find nesting in our four seater outhouse." So I went to the john carrying my .45 with me. Fortunately there were no snakes. Before I left Pop and his Military Government, I borrowed a typewriter and wrote a letter to friends and family detailing the reunion. As you can see from the letter, the commander edited it liberally before it went out. (see illustration on following pages)

I got on a troop carrier plane and flew back to Manila. There was a band playing, high dignitaries waiting, and I thought, "This can't be for me, what is this?" They were expecting Japanese high-ranking officers to come in that day to discuss terms of a peace negotiation after the explosion of the second atomic bomb and they were quite disappointed when a scruffy lieutenant stepped off the plane rather than Japanese generals, so they scooted me out of there.

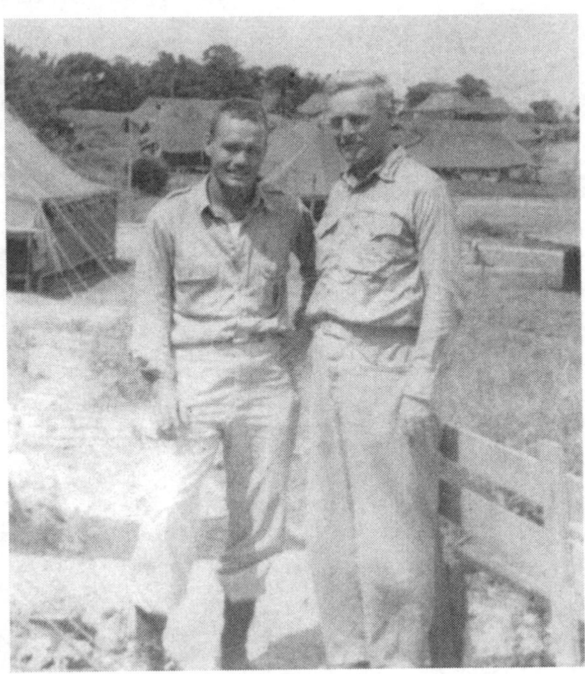

Somewhere on Okinawa
Saturday, Aug 18

Dear Gang,

The millenium has arrived! After tracking "Slippery Mose" Firman 10,000 miles, Win "always gets his man" Firman finally caught up with him in that garden spot of the turbulent Pacific, Okinawa. The great man-hunter utilized a fast plane from Manila to catch the old fox in his lair. (Incidentally the reception I got on popping into the Commander's office was something like that accorded a second-hand book salesman or the Federal Bureau of Internal Revenue). After convincing Pop that it was really his long lost son, father of his first two grandchildren (the handle-bar mustache confused him but only momentarily - i.e. two days) we set out to do the island. And that we did. First of course introductions to every man, woman and dog on the island (Dad can never forget his boyhood ambition to be a politician so he peddled me like black market nylons), then a "bull" session such as no one who is not a, or has not lived with a, or who has not known intimately a FIRMAN could ever conceive of.

By noon we were about done lying to each other about our parts in "gloriously bringing the titanic world conflict to a victorious termination" and after chow which plainly indicated to me why the Commander's shorts fit me like a ready-made barracks bag we stoumbled on two sheep waiting to be fleeced. Said the Army (that's me) in oily tones "How about a friendly little game of bridge at say a tenth of a cent?" Said his partner in chicanery and skullduggery in dulcet tones "Oh, make it a quarter cent - we might as well lose all our money." When Dad and I had stopped laughing at this last brilliant irony we settled down to make the innocents regret they ever left that glorious man of war, in the Hudson, - the "Prairie State". At the end of an hour or so Father and Son emerged winners to the tune of $8 each - the truth so help us - only catch was that the losers paid off in Yen which are only good on Okinawa so Pop generously took all the winnings (of course he hadn't figured that out in advance - oh, no!)

In the afternoon the old man put in just enough time at his desk (reading New Yorker) so that he can claim a full day's pay and then we took off in a jeep to go swimming. What a

Handwritten margin notes:
Ha Ha!
First time I ever heard Win called a "millenium"
Handle-bar! It looks like a Lonesome Fuller brush.
The dogs all said "Hello"
But didn't have any feminine customers, damn it.
Three times got a word in edgewise!
Speak for yourself, louse!
Libel I'm slim as a reed.
"Me and Doug"
His money being no good who would have paid losses. He didn't figure that out Dohdro,
Sister Libel!

beach - the Coney Island of the West. We had a helluva swell time making like seals and submarines and got back in time for some real American whiskey (supplied, however, by one of the politician's ward-heelers). Then chow in seven courses and afterwards a friendly little poker game until ten. (Seven officers and the stakes were 5, 10 and 20 cents.) For a long time Messers Firman were not acquitting themselves in the true Amherst tradition. In fact starting the last hand of the evening I was $4 down and "the fair haired windbag" was only a few bux up. But I was dealing and Pop suggested double ante and I called it high-low and we really went to work. The Commander was sailing into the high hand and I was a cinch for the low hand so we bumped that old pot back and forth while the other five just threw their money down the sewer. When we split the pot (high hand gets half and low hand gets the other half) there were eight dollars in it - biggest haul of the evening. So I came out even (actually won 75¢ which the old man confiscated using the gag that Yen were no good to me on Luzon) and the Navy end of the family made another eight iron men. Not a bad day's haul. After that we sacked up and today have not started to fleece the flock yet. More later.

!!!! I never. They've messed the other four

Of course the whiskey had him seeing triple.

And to think his high school yearbook called him "a mother's pride - a father's joy"!

Is he calling me a sewer?

You ought to see what he bought at the PX with my good yen.

A moment of silence to hear the eagle scream.

All my love,

Ken

P.S. Coming up here wasthe best idea I had since I got married - this is a real vacation for me and Dad should survive it.

Open to some argument

He still thinks that was a good idea, Julie.

1st Endorsement:

I concur in the non-libelous portions of basic communication, and changes are pending on the balance. He is as fresh as ever, and has considerably lowered my dignity. However, I'm proud as hell to have him here, and you'll all note how quick the Japs gave up when two Firmans got together. The mighty atoms!

"Pop"

The Army spells it with an "i" but I'm in the Navy, thank God!

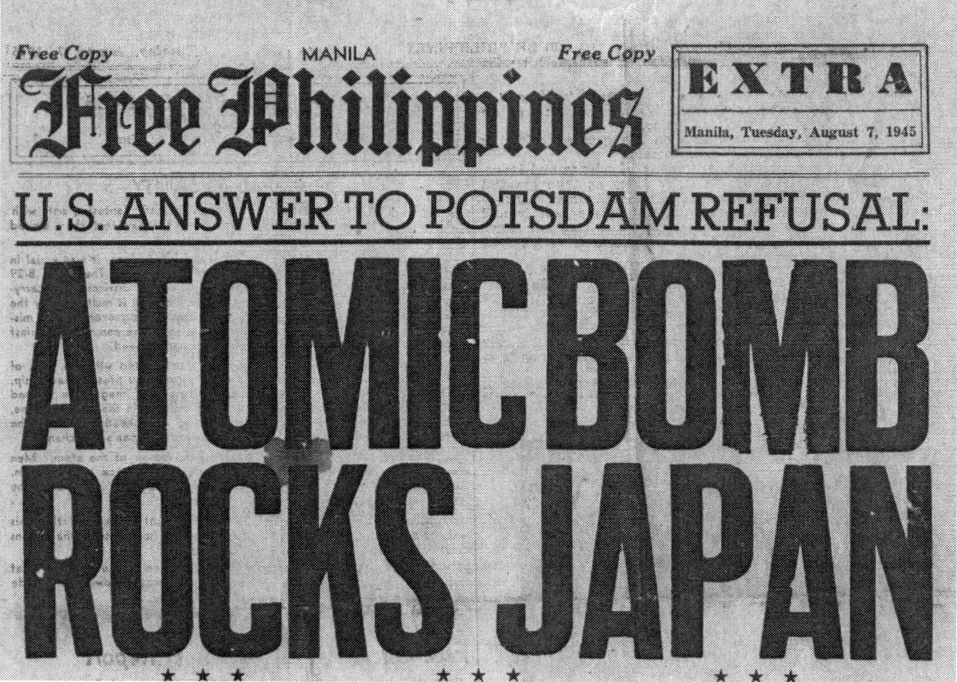

Free Copy MANILA Free Copy

Free Philippines

EXTRA

Manila, Tuesday, August 7, 1945

U.S. ANSWER TO POTSDAM REFUSAL:

ATOMIC BOMB ROCKS JAPAN

Chapter Nineteen

THE ATOMIC BOMB AND THE BEGINNING OF THE END OF THE WAR

On August 6th, the atomic bomb had been dropped on Hiroshima and August 8th, another bomb was dropped on Nagasaki when the Japanese refused to be convinced by the first dreadful bomb. The mood in the military, especially in bomb disposal was hopeful. We knew bombs and this seemed like the bombs that would bring a swift end to the war. In fact, though, we had little idea, at the time, of the utter devastation that these bombs had caused and would continue to cause. We did wonder about that kind of bomb though—not something we knew anything about! When I was discussing the atomic bombs with several other bomb disposal officers, I said, "I sure am glad that both of them went off, I would hate to be called upon to defuze an atomic bomb." One of the officers said, "What difference does it make? Whether you're working on a 98 pound parafrag bomb that goes off, you're just as dead as when an atomic bomb goes off while you're working on it." True enough, but I'm still glad I never had to defuze one of those. In fact, I hope the world never sees another one of those dropped.

A good day in bomb disposal

Chapter Twenty

BUT NOT OVER YET

The war had ended on August 15, but our work was not done. Especially in bomb disposal, the military would be actively engaged for quite awhile, while the world began to adjust to peace. Such was the case for me. On August 24 we got a call that a duck (an amphibious vehicle, actually DUKW, but pronounced *duck)* carrying three 2,000 pound bombs had smashed into a truck. Would we come out and get the bombs so a wrecker could haul in the two vehicles? I took one man and, with red light flashing, we burned up the road to the scene of the wreck. Traffic was backed up for half a mile. We backed in and the wrecking truck lifted the one-ton bombs into our truck.

We braced them and took them out to the Air Corps bomb dump. I rode in the back of our truck and tried to keep the bombs from rolling. Quite a job dodging three tons of bombs. When we got to the dump there was no crane operator so we first tried rolling them off the back but the carrying lugs stopped us—then we tried backing the truck at top speed and jamming on the brakes to throw them out but that failed, too. Just about then the crane operator returned and picked up the bombs as if they were babies. Problem solved.

It is mentioned in the weekly activity report for 20 August, which I have included for background material on our duties.

208th ORDNANCE BOMB DISPOSAL SQUAD
Base R, AFWESPAC, APO 73

WF/rcr
27 Aug 1945

SUBJECT: Bomb Disposal Activities.

TO : ORDNANCE OFFICER, Headquarters, Base R, AFWESPAC, APO 73.

1. In compliance with verbal orders your Hqrs., the following report is submitted covering this Units activities for the period 20 Aug thru 26 Aug 45.

2 armed US Fuzes picked up in QM Laundry area.

US fragmentation grenade was reported to be on side of road leading to BAUAN. Same was found and taken to Ammo Dump.

2 US grenades were picked up at S-2.

3 - 2000 lb US bombs were taken out of a wrecked Duck (DUKW). Accident occured approximately 2200 23 Aug 45 on the BAUAN Raad. Bombs were loaded on this Units truck and taken to the 1909th Air Corps Bomb Dump.

2 US Mark series incindiary bombs were picked up at S-2. They were examined for explosive matter then returned.

Picked up 4 US 20 lb frag bombs with AN-M 110 Nose fuzes at 842d Ord. C.

Went to scene of Ammo fire at Control Tower by the beach and inspected area for dangerous objects. Removed 2 frag grenades, 2 rifle grenades, and 3 trip flares.

Inspected 4.5 Rocket (US) which was unfuzed and inserted in Rocket tube at the Base R. Ordnance Supply Depot. Also defuzed and removed 2 US 23 lb parafrag bombs with AN-M 120 nose fuze from same area.

Picked up 1 US 75 mm white phospherous round from the 867th Engineers. Round was taken to Base R Ammo Dump.

Lt. Firman lectured to the Philippine B.D. Squads in Manila on 21 Aug 45. They were being trained under MEIU.

Removed from a cave at the 11th Airborne Area in LIPA the following. 3 cases TNT, 5 cases chain explosive in haversack cases, 1 case M 49 Trip flares, 1½ cases smoke grenades, 3 cases frag grenades, 1 case anti-personnel mines M2A1, 10 bangalore torpedoes, 9 HE 81 mm mortars, 2 WP 81 mm mortars, 30 rockets, heat M6A1, 8 boxes #8 electric blasting caps, 1 case of mixed booby traps and igniters (pull, release, pressure), and 2 chains of demolition blocks, M1 (tetrytol).

WINFIELD FIRMAN
2d Lt. Ord. Dept.
Commanding

On 25 September I received this commendation just before my promotion:

HEADQUARTERS BASE R
UNITED STATES ARMY FORCES WESTERN PACIFIC
Office of the S-2

APO 73
25 September 1945

SUBJECT: Commendation

TO : Second Lieutenant Winfield Firman, O-1558456, Ordnance, Commanding, 208th Bomb Disposal Squad, Base R, APO 73

It is my pleasure as Assistant Executive, S-2, Headquarters, Base R, to offer my appreciation and commendation to you as Commanding Officer of the 208th Bomb Disposal Squad, for your efforts in behalf of technical intelligence activities of this base from the period 25 July 1945 to 1 September 1945. Although you were occupied with the normal activities of your squad, you willingly and voluntarily took upon yourself the task of collecting and deactivating many types of Japanese shells and fuzes to be used for instructional or display purposes. Your activities in connection with the searching out, location and disposition of dangerous Japanese explosives not only resulted in the uncovering of material of intelligence value, but also removed a definite and serious hazard to the lives of American troops and Filipinos. Your work has been of material benefit to the S-2 Office of this base.

Philip J. Lawrence
PHILIP J. LAWRENCE
Captain, Infantry
Ass't. Exec., S-2

Later on, in September, I was awarded the bronze star. Essentially it was for all the work I'd been doing, but they picked out a couple of incidents in order to make up the background for the citation. I had just been made a First Lieutenant three days earlier, coincident with this commendation to Second Lieutenant Firman, so this was a happy couple of days and I couldn't wait to telegraph my sweet wife Julie about the big news. Obviously, the bronze star meant five points towards my coming home, so that was a plus.

HEADQUARTERS
PHILIPPINE BASE SECTION
UNITED STATES ARMY
SERVICES OF
SUPPLY

CITATION

TO ACCOMPANY THE AWARD OF THE
BRONZE STAR MEDAL PER GENERAL
ORDERS NO. 118, 28 SEPTEMBER 1945

Second Lieutenant WINFIELD FIRMAN, 01558456, Ordnance Department, United States Army. For meritorious achievement in direct support of combat operations against the enemy at San Fernando, Pampanga, and Batangas, Batangas, Philippines, from 12 July 1945 to 14 August 1945. As the Commanding Officer of a Bomb Disposal Squad, Second Lieutenant FIRMAN was responsible for the successful execution of many missions that were beyond the normal call of duty of his unit. These missions included the inspection, classification, and disassembly of captured enemy material in order to furnish Headquarters Intelligence Sections with technical data of value in combat operations. On 12 July 1945 a B-24 bomber loaded with twelve fuzed two hundred and sixty pound fragmentation bombs crashed near San Fernando, The impact of the crash had thrown high octane gasoline over the entire area creating imminent danger of fire and explosions. Second Lieutenant FIRMAN with utter disregard for his own personal safety, entered the wreckage and unfuzed the two bombs that were fixed in the plane, cleared the area of spectators and deactivated the scattered bombs. When his unit was called upon to destroy three sunken enemy ammunition barges, which constituted a menace to shipping off the coast of Mindoro, he unhesitatingly accepted the assignment although he knew the risk involved, as he lacked the proper diving equipment. With the aid of an enlisted member of his unit, Second Lieutenant FIRMAN dived repeatedly to a depth of twenty feet until the detonating charges were affixed and the barges successfully destroyed. His personal conduct and leadership under hazardous conditions were an inspiration to the members of his unit and reflect the highest credit upon himself and upon the military service.

Home address: Mrs. Juliet Firman (Wife)
18 Circle Road,
Scarsdale, New York.

BY COMMAND OF MAJOR GENERAL PLANK:

S. A. MARCINKO
Lt. Col., AGD
Adjutant General

On September 29th, 1945, we were called out for some bombs that the officer of the unit did not recognize. We met out there and found that there were a whole flock of butterfly bombs in their bivouac area. The bombs, with anti-disturbance fuzes, were probably one of the most dangerous of all bombs. It's a small bomb, but many British bomb disposal men lost their lives to that bomb. Captain Q., just in from Italy, lost one of his men, who had been overseas for only thirty-two days. The kid was using a mine detector in tall grass when he happened to nudge one of these bombs and it went off.

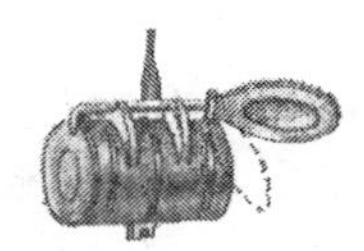

1 2-KG. "BUTTERFLY" BOMB (VANES CLOSED)

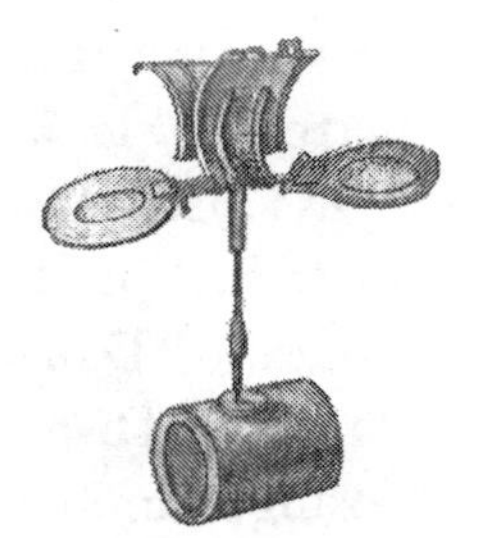

2 2-KG. "BUTTERFLY" BOMB (VANES OPEN)

The 2 kg, or 4¼ pound butterfly bomb was originated by the Germans to drop over allied airfields when the Germans were planning to come in for a strike. The bombs were carried in containers, as many as 80 of the bombs in the canister, which would blow open with a small black powder fuse after it was dropped, and these 80 bombs would spread out over a wide area. The problem with them was that they contained three different fuzes. One third of the bombs had impact fuzes, so they would go off, detonating four-plus pounds of explosive, which is not that much, but it digs a pretty good crater in an airfield. One third of the bombs had time delay fuzes, so that you never knew when you found one how much time was left before it went off. Normally that delay was probably no more than a few hours and designed to discourage personnel from picking the bomb up on discovering it. The third type of fuze in the remaining third of the bombs was an anti-disturbance fuze, which after landing, would release a little clockwork mechanism, so that if it were picked up, it would set off the anti-disturbance fuze and the bomb. As you would guess, this had pretty disastrous results. The bomb was so successful that the U.S. Air Force copied it and dropped a lot of these on Japanese positions on the islands. And this is what we came across. Our first butterfly bombs. More than a month after the war had ended, we faced our greatest danger.

As I say, Captain Q. had lost one of his men without even realizing that there were any bombs in the tall grass. Incidentally, the Captain tells me that he is one of the 15 bomb disposal officers who had squads with the 5th army and he is one of only three survivors: quite a poor percentage, quite a sad story. Anyway, we couldn't move these bombs because all of them were now armed with an anti-disturbance fuze. So, we cleared out the entire area, asking men to leave and to take their vehicles with them. Then we sandbagged the seven bombs that were spread over 100 yards, placed half a pound of TNT, packed with mud, on each bomb, put an electric blasting cap in each block of TNT, and connected the entire set-up to one circuit. Finally, we took off a good distance, trailing our combat wire behind us, then twisted the detonator. BANG!! The seven bombs blew simultaneously, in as neat a job as I've ever seen. All we could find of the sandbags were small scraps, but they did the trick of preventing fragmentation and no installation in the vicinity was even slightly damaged. That's the first time I, or any of the squad, had seen any of these bombs. An interesting job. The War Department Manual I first read in 2010 said, "IF FOUND UNEXPLODED, THIS BOMB SHOULD NOT BE DISTURBED, AS THIS FUZE IS SENSITIVE WHEN ARMED." One of the most disturbing episodes in "Danger: UXB"—a great movie by the way—is with the British Bomb Disposal taking out or blowing up scores of these bombs—and losing a number of men in doing so.

As I wrote, a bomb disposal squad had a T/O (Table of Organization) of one officer and six non-commissioned officers (sergeants and corporals). Wherever possible, a squad was attached to a large unit—generally a battalion or a base command—for rations and quarters. We would hear reveille sound at our host unit and we would fall out and mimic them. I would shout, "Battalion, Ten-Hut," followed by, "Report." In rotation, each of six men would salute and report "Company A all present or accounted for," "Company B all present or accounted for," and when company F had reported we would fall out laughing. Humor in wartime. Not very funny, but we enjoyed the mimicry.

Another interesting experience on Batangas was when we were blowing up a couple of 250 lb. U.S. bombs. We hooked up a detonator to the bombs and checked the entire vicinity to make sure there was no one there. After a last look to see if the coast was clear and shouting our standard warning, "Fire in the hole!" we blew them up. As we got up from our hiding places, what met our eyes was a Filipino walking along about 50 yards from the explosion. What a scare that gave us. Fortunately, the deep ravine sent the blast upwards so when he came walking out of the woods just as we detonated the bombs, it only hit him with a cloud of smoke. I have enclosed the October military history as it catches the variety of our work.

1 Nov 1945

MILITARY HISTORY
1 Oct 45 to 31 Oct 45

In early October an LCT was placed at the disposal of this Unit for the purpose of dumping at sea the contents of the Ammo Dump maintained by the Squad. All explosive material was trucked to the ship, stowed and carried to the Verde Island Straits where it was dumped overboard. The materiel included hundreds of tons of Jap projectiles, over two hundred Jap bombs, cases of fuzes, land mines, loose powder, knee mortars, and thousand of rounds of Jap small arms ammo. Also disposed of were 14 U.S. 250 lb. bombs, 16 U.S. parafrag bombs, and a large quantity of U.S. 155 H.E. projectiles.

Other activities carried out by this Unit during the month included the investigation of an explosion on BATANGAS BEACH which injured 14 persons, checking several caves in back of Base R Headquarters for booby-traps, removing booby-traps from vehicles stored at the Ordnance Depot (this matter is being investigated by S-2 for possible sabotage), checking a shipload of bombs and fuzes which had been damaged in a series of typhoons the ship had weathered at Okinawa, removing a large store of explosives found in a Canning Factory at LIPA, disposing of 7 Jap bombs found in LIPA, and defuzing and removing over a dozen U.S. 23 lb. parafrag bombs reported in various Units throughout Base R installations.

The remainder of the work was of a routine nature such as the disposal of several thousand rounds of machine-gun ammunition, the removal of cases of TNT, blasting caps, spools of primacord, fragmentation and smoke grenades and a case of bomb fuzes (the latter found on an Army Transport).

The Commanding Officer was awarded the Bronze Star Medal per General Order #118, PHIBSEC. T/5 John L. Hefner, the Squad demolition non-com, was transferred to the 141st Bomb Disposal Squad which was moving to Japan - this was done in order to put an experienced man in the 141st Squad which had suffered a complete personnel turnover due to men returning to the States on points.

WINFIELD FIRMAN
1st Lt. Ord. Dept.
Commanding

Cpl. Lisiecki playing "wild west."

Win with a bigger "gun."

Chapter Twenty-one

THE WAR IS OVER, BUT NOT FOR ME

In late November of '45, I went to the AFWESPAC (American Forces, Western Pacific) Ordnance Offices. The officer in charge told me our squad's deactivation day was April 15th, but said he had no way of rebuilding my squad, now down to three non-commissioned officers, with the other three ready to be discharged. Nor were there any new bomb disposal squads to replace mine. To illustrate my difficulties I enclose an excerpt from a letter to Julie:

...the rest of the day trying to line up new men for the squad. I met every conceivable obstacle before I got one definite from the 377th, one tentative from the 842nd and one each possible from the 3427th and the 928th. Despite the fact that all those C.O.'s are my buddies they just don't have men to spare. That is why I hit each of them for just one man. I certainly hope I get a clerk in that bunch because 45 pointers are due to leave early in January which means that Biehl with his 59 and Robbie and Marie with their 54 will be leaving in the next month. Still nothing new on officers—the 73 pointers just went on orders. There is a tremendous shortage of officers. We are 12 shy in the Battalion and will be about 15 shy by the first of Dec. Tough deal, that's for sure.

So I began enticing men to train as B.D. soldiers with the non-commissioned officer's rank and the much greater freedom in very small units as the attraction. When the 208th bomb disposal squad was ordered to New Guinea in late December, I had recruited and trained three soldiers but had lost two on points for discharge. The remaining three members of the 208th bomb disposal squad, as I had predicted, were all sent home before we left for New Guinea. So, off to New Guinea I went, with three replacements who had no real experience in disarming and blowing up bombs, artillery shells, and miscellaneous explosives.

The army "send home" point system which stripped me of my entire bomb disposal squad went like this:

Points were used near the end of the war to determine in what order soldiers were allowed to go home.

1. Service Credit – One point for each month of Army service since 16, September 1940.
2. Overseas Credit – One point for each month served overseas since 16, September 1940.
3. Parenthood Credit – Twelve points for each child under 18 up to a limit of three children.
4. Combat Credit – Five points for each award of combat decorations since 16, September 1940.

Combat credits, The War Department said, will be based on awards of the Distinguished Service Cross, the Legion of Merit, the Silver Star, the Soldier's Medal, the Bronze Star, the Air Medal, the Purple Heart and Bronze Service Stars for participation in battle.

By December '45, my point total was 68—32 for months of service, 7 for months overseas, 5 for the bronze star, and 24 for two dependent children. And even though this exceeded the 65 necessary for a lieutenant to go home (70 for a captain, 75 for a major), the army had no compunctions about assigning me to New Guinea.

It might be useful to give some idea of the type of thing we were working on, picking up, blowing up, taking to sea, before going off to New Guinea.

On one occasion, we picked up 231 cases of Japanese 105 mm high explosive projectiles, 57 cases of 150 mm high explosives, 90 cases of 75 mm high explosive shells, 246 loose rounds of 150 mm projectiles, 388 loose rounds of 105 mm projectiles, 109 loose rounds of U.S. 155 mm high explosive projectiles, 24 rounds of 75 mm shells, 70 miscellaneous Japanese projectiles, 1800 rounds of .50 caliber ammo, 36 Japanese 50 mm mortar projectiles, 143 miscellaneous fuzes, 4 boxes of loose explosive powder, 2 Japanese 15 kg concrete bombs, 24 Japanese navy 250 kg AP bombs (armor piercing), 2 Japanese army 250 kg GP (general purpose) bombs, and 1 100 kg GP bomb.

As you can see, this was typical of the work we were doing, running into many thousand rounds of artillery shells, grenades, rockets, and bombs ranging from 50 kg (110 pounds) to giants at 1000 kg (2200 pounds). These tons and tons of high explosives had to be destroyed by detonation in a wide open area, or, more often, loaded onto barges to be towed by a tugboat to deep water for dumping.

A G-2 report on November 13 said a naval mine had been found in a bay some distance away and requested we dispose of it. This was the first request I had refused since arriving in the Philippines. A naval mine just recently killed another bomb disposal officer, whom I had known pretty well, a class behind me at Aberdeen. Actually, that was not part of our work because, where we spend about half a day studying naval mines, the navy gives an eight-week course on mine disposal to selected officers.

Intended to sink ships, naval mines are huge and can be detonated by any number of fuzes—anti-sound, anti-metal, anti-disturbance. My fellow bomb disposal officer found a naval mine on the beach. Cautioning his squad to remain well back, he approached the mine after removing his belt, watch, and sidearm. As he got close to the mine, its tonnage of explosives went off, killing him instantly. What happened? No one is sure. Speculation had Japanese soldiers (sailors?) detonating the mine from the bushes. As I said before, we were not trained to handle naval mines nor did we have the tools. So, "Sorry, we can't dispose of your mine."

I got a call from the ammo officer at Base X telling me about a big explosion and telling me where I could pick up the stuff that didn't go off (Base X is in Manila), and then a few minutes later I was called over to the office of the Ordnance Officer, Major Curtis, to be introduced to a colonel in the MP's who had come down to tell me about the same incident. So we borrowed a big truck, picked up ten Filipinos, and took off right after lunch in the weapons carrier and the borrowed truck. It was way out in Laguna Province and what a mess! It had been a Japanese ammo dump right in a village and the natives had been industriously chipping the picric acid out of the projectiles (150 mm) for explosives for fishing. They must have been doing it for weeks because we found a slew of the empty projectiles. Finally, one went off and set off what we estimate to be at least 50 others. The explosion completely destroyed four houses, blasted a huge crater, killed 11 people and injured 5 more, killed dogs and pigs, and the blast effect tore the fronts out of the houses across the street. It resembled nothing so much as the pictures you see of a ravaged European village. The stench was terrible and dogs were eating dead pigs. The colonel told us that earlier in the day, the dogs had been eating the dead people, but they had been removed. We immediately went to work with our labor gang and cleaned out all the remaining explosives. In the ruins of one hut they had built a fireplace of these projectiles!!! It is incredible, isn't it? But the explosives mean fish, and fish mean they won't starve, so it just seems to them to be gambling their lives to be sure of living. A sad circle. The colonel stopped by as we were finishing the job and asked me to submit a full report to him so he could close the investigation.

208TH ORDNANCE BOMB DISPOSAL SQUAD
Sub Base R, AFWESPAC, APO 73

WF/pms
11 Dec 1945

Subject: Explosion of Japanese Ammunition at Alaminos
To : Provincial Commander MPC, Leguna Province, Santa Cruz APO 501

1. In compliance with verbal request your headquarters, an investigation was made by this unit of the explosion of Japanese 150 mm HE projectiles which reputedly killed eleven Filipinos and injured five. The investigation disclosed the following facts:

a) The natives in the barrio had, for some time, been chipping the picric acid from this abandoned Japanese ammunition to use for fishing. There is ample proof of this in as much as this unit removed 43 unexploded shells, most of which were completely free of explosive matter, from the scene of the accident.

b) The explosion of one of these projectiles (probably in a deteriorated condition) due to this chipping action fired, by sympathetic detonation, an estimated 40 to 50 additional fully loaded projectiles. This estimate is based on the size of the crater (7 ft deep and 20 ft across) and the terrific destruction which included a high toll in human and animal life, the complete leveling of four native houses, and the caving in of the fronts of houses across the road due to blast effects.

c) It was also found that the natives were using these projectiles in the construction of fireplaces in their houses and, while it is assumed these were all empty projectiles, it is none the less very difficult to remove all the picric acid clinging to the projectile walls.

d) Undoubtedly, this explosion is due to the failure of the people of this barrio to notify proper authorities of the presence of these explosives and their attempts to remove explosives contained in these projectiles for their own use. It is the opinion of the undersigned that the United States Army has no liability in the matter.

Subsequent to this investigation, this unit, at the request of the mayor of Alaminos, removed over two tons of miscellaneous explosives (bombs, rockets, and projectiles) from Alaminos and vicinity.

WINFIELD FIRMAN
1st Lt. Ord. Dept.
Commanding

Copies to: Ord. Officer Sub-base R
S-2 Sub-base R
Ammunition Officer Base X
Bomb Disposal Officer AFWESPAC

I also hoped to be able to start a minor crusade through the Filipino Military Police to warn the natives of the tremendous risk involved in fooling with that stuff or keeping it lying around. Incidentally, the colonel told us he had been stationed in Laguna Province 25 years ago—I figured that would be about the time that MacArthur's father had been Commander-In-Chief here and he confirmed my guess.

Chapter twenty-two

OFF TO NEW GUINEA

On November 12, 1945, we received orders to fly to Finschhafen, 2,000 miles from Batangas. At that time I had only three members of my squad: Sergeant Nanney, Corporal Lisiecki and Corporal Schroeder. We originally had six in the bomb disposal squad but one was transferred to lend some experience to a bomb disposal squad going to Japan, and three others had enough points to go home. I was busily trying to recruit members from other ammo ordnance units to rebuild the squad when, at the last moment, my corporal, who had handled all of my correspondence and all of the reports, Robbie, was transferred out, as was Sergeant St. Marie, as they had enough points to go home. So, I was left with three new recruits who I had been busily training. I was unable to get the other three squad members that I needed because so many men were going home, and so few wanted to hook up with a bomb disposal squad. So off we went to New Guinea, a lieutenant and three non-commissioned officers, all of whom, with the exception of the lieutenant, were brand new to bomb disposal. And expected to remove huge amounts of burned ammunition and bombs in Finschhafen.

The four of us went to Manila clutching our orders in our hands. After four days of the inevitable confusion, we found ourselves on an Australian courier plane at five A.M. Just missed meal stops at Leyte and Morotai. Next, we stopped at Viak, completing the first day of our

2,000-mile jaunt. Engine trouble brought a stop at Hollandia and we arrived at Finschhafen just too late for dinner on the second day. Now, six meals are about four too many to miss. So I asked what was available and they referred me to a small PX, only to find they wanted dollars, not pesos. So, with a hundred dollars of pesos in my pocket, I had to bum a buck from a fellow officer and rush back to the PX before it closed for the night.

December 22 we cased the big ammunition fire that we had come to clean up. Roughly six or eight thousand burned, battered but unexploded projectiles that are left of what must have been a beautiful series of explosions. They say the explosions lasted for six hours and I saw where they had fired a smaller dump over a mile away. We didn't start the job because we were informed that a more pressing job awaited us at Lae, 55 miles down the coast. We were to be flown there the next day but the plane got away without us because the orders hadn't been cut, because the ordnance officer hadn't put in a request, because he wasn't sure, because, etc. So, in the afternoon we took a truck with three of us working on the ground, one man on the truck, and loaded 300 rounds, about 4 ½ tons in an hour.

We took it as it came without segregating the so-called "dangerous" projectiles, the ones having actually been blown about, burned in the fires and explosions, which had to be handled very carefully. And we also handled all of the bombs that had not been burned or partially exploded. We trucked all the explosives to a barge for disposal at sea. This busy little afternoon completely upset all theories but mine, which is, given 40 men and four trucks, I would get that junk out of there in four days. The ordnance officer and the ammo officer estimated it would take 3-4 weeks, even using native labor. Then they asked me how long it would take me if we couldn't get any help and I said, "We won't do it. If the base commander isn't interested enough in the job to give us help, we won't do it because it is not our work to begin with and four of us would take a month to do it. I'll just radio Afwespac for orders to return."

As I pointed out, Christmas in New Guinea was not the greatest place in the world. As they say, "New Guinea is a swell place to be FROM." Also, "I got skinny in New Guinea, Papa. There's malaria in the area in Swapa, Papa." (*Swapa* stands for Southwest Asia/Pacific Area).

And I count myself lucky that I spent merely one Christmas Day overseas, whereas my brothers Roy, Joe, and Bill each spent two or three over there. I was saddened on reading this brief poem while I was in New Guinea at Christmastime. It was sixty-five years later when my daughter found it had been written by Francis Quarles in, astoundingly, 1632.

> **Our God and soldiers we alike adore ev'n at the brink of danger; not before: After deliverance, both alike requited, Our God's forgotten, and our soldiers slighted.**

Finally the squad was flown to Lae to inspect the huge job waiting to be done there—clean out fourteen badly damaged ammunition dumps. On our first trip from Finschhafen to Lae—perhaps fifty-five miles—our old C-47 (a twin-engined workhorse used for many years by the allies) flown by Aussie pilots had to return to Finsch three times because of engine trouble. The short hop was over hostile mountains and desolate countryside so it was always heart stopping when the plane had to turn back. In our subsequent flights to and from Lae, three times out of four the beat up C-47 had trouble and had to return to the airfield from which we had started. My three squad members and I should have gotten used to the frequent engine problems but it continued to be nerve-wracking until we finally left New Guinea for good.

As I wrote to Julie on December 24, Lae was not a garden spot.

It is inhabited by field mice which carry sleeping sickness, typhus ticks, and swarms of flies and mosquitoes. Also a sprinkling of very black natives for whom their sole garment is a brightly colored cloth skirt (male and female). They add war paint and a bone in their nose when they do anything important such as digging drainage ditches for the 'Yonkee Dollair.' They are the original fuzzy-wuzzies and quite frightening till one corners you and, as you gasp out a last prayer, he blandly says, 'You sell me bicycle, huh, Mike? No have? Then give me chooin gum.'

After the squad had flown back to Finsch from Lae and begun work on the ammunition dump destroyed by fire and explosions, it was decided by the Base Commanding Officer that all work in the American installation at Finsch would be subordinated to the job of removing or destroying the thousands of bombs left behind by the American Air Force at Lae. Hence, the squad immediately flew back to Lae and with the aid of a small group of New Guinea natives, and using every truck available, began the tremendous job of cleaning up the fourteen bomb dumps between Lae and Nadzap.

The dumps at Nadzap were sufficiently removed from the main roads to allow destruction by demolition. And using explosives furnished by the Royal Australian Engineers, my unit blew up over 6,600,-23 pound parafrag bombs, 23-500 pound bombs and a lot of miscellaneous things. The remaining dumps were too close to the main road to detonate their explosives and their contents had to be hauled by truck for distances up to eighteen miles to a barge in the main harbor. The barge was twice towed to sea by an Australian tug and all the bombs and artillery shells were dropped in the water.

One of the interesting facts of being in Lae was that a hop, skip, and jump away was the Australian Officer's Club, which was a rare treat for me. As an American officer I was allowed in and when we would go over there for dinner, which was four shillings or 64 cents, we would have to check our sidearms at the coat check office. It was pretty funny because I was then carrying a carbine. I checked this and saw here in the coat check room at the club, hundreds of sidearms being checked. With the Japanese not too far away, I asked my host, "What would happen if the Japanese broke through the line and we were having dinner at the Australian Officer's Club?" He said it would be pandemonium as we all rushed up and said, "Here's my check, where's my sidearm?" And it would have been—but it did not happen. I was happy because the meal was good, we could get a cocktail for a shilling and this was the best food I had had since I had gone to war.

The Aussie troops had a good sense of humor. In one disputed sector there was a sign reading, "No kibitzers allowed past this point." The other side of the sign read, "No Japs allowed past this point."

Returning to Finschhafen by plane, the squad took a look at the huge ammunition dump there. I said to the commanding officer, "We can't do it without some help." Because native laborers were not available, we decided that it would be totally impossible, between now and World War III, for four of us to take all the explosives out of this several acre large bomb dump that had been burned. I told the commanding officer of the base that we were going to return to Batangas and he said, "Oh no. We will provide you with help." The following day was rainy and twenty surly G.I.'s showed up. We found that these G.I.'s were very unhappy, as they had been doing no work whatsoever, for so long, that the prospect of being recruited into our little group had them all twitching before we started. Several of them were corporals or sergeants. Then it began to rain out there and they promptly wanted to quit, which I would not let them do. I had never been allowed to quit work when it rained, as either an enlisted man or even as an officer, and I was darned if I was going to waste another whole day. I got just as drenched as they did working right alongside of them while doing twice as much as they did. Well, they complained and grumbled and swore, and all in all put on the poorest show I've ever seen. Bigger crybabies would be hard to find. So after clearing only four truckloads, which took about an hour and a half, I sent them all home.

When I got back and got my clothes changed, I went to see their respective C.O.'s, the situation was so ludicrous! The G.I.'s went to their commanding officers and told them the job was hazardous, whining about working in the rain and swore they would take a court-martial before they went back. I told them that their men were lazy, chronic complainers and practically useless. This made the captain and lieutenant, whose men we had been using, madder than they were when I came in, and we really went at each other. I told them the job was an ordnance job and the men, by the strange system prevalent in the army, cannot select what jobs they will do, or won't do, and if I were the commanding officer, I would court-martial a few of them to call their bluff. But here officers seem to be afraid to speak crossly to an enlisted man, work them long or hard, or take any chances at all with their precious skins. Almost to the point where the officers were taking orders from the men. I had an appointment to see the base commander the next day to have the question settled. If he issued the order that the G.I.'s must do the work, fine. If he decided both native labor and G.I.'s are out of the question, we would pack up and get out of there. Nothing would have suited me better. But the Commanding Officer said, "Oh no, you don't get away that easy, I will have some help for you tomorrow." The help turned out to be 30 Japanese P.O.W.'s who were delighted to get out of their prison camp and to be doing something, even if that "something" including picking up rounds of ammunition that had been burned.

In the next couple of days, the Japanese and my three men picked up 40,000 artillery rounds undamaged in the fire in the dump. We also uncovered 13,525 burned and damaged rounds and these were hauled by truck to barges and later dumped at sea. The Japanese P.O.W.s really enjoyed the chance to get out of the camp for a day or two, and we had hundreds of volunteers, many of whom happily joined us and never gave a thought to the hazardous duty. They had great fun with fuzes, which they learned to take out of the artillery shells and throw through the air, and the fuze would go off with a bang when it would hit the ground. This constantly startled all of us but it tickled them. The Japanese helped us load thousands of rounds onto barges and a number of them even went out with us to help dump them overboard. There were rats on the barges and the Japanese loved to play soccer with the them, eventually kicking them overboard. They were a happy group, even though we could not understand each other. They were hardworking and really making a huge contribution to our war effort. Question: Is it in keeping with the Geneva Convention to ask P.O.W.s to do hazardous duty like this?—I don't know. The Japanese did not seem to care and they really did a fine job while enjoying themselves.

My clerk, Corporal Lisiecki, and I spent much of New Year's Day catching up on neglected reports, among them: seven *Morning Reports*, seven *Daily Strength Reports*, one *Weekly Strength Report*, one *Strength and Status Report*, a *Status of Vehicles Report*, *Other Ordnance Major Items Report*, an *Atabrine Report*, a *Weapons Showdown Report*, the *Activities Report*, the *Historical Summary* and a *Vehicle Mileage Report*. What would the Army ever do without these reports? They are overlapping, most are unnecessary, and I am certain 98.6% are never read.

From a letter to Julie January 8, 1946:

Another busy day in the salt mines. Sgt. Nanney had to go to the hospital first to have a shell fragment removed from his eye—gotten while we were working yesterday. Then we jeeped to the dump and put in a hard morning's work to be followed by our usual swim of one hour's duration—a delightful innovation which we must carry back to Luzon with us. Then C rations heated in the sun and they don't seem bad when you get as hungry as we do. The menu today was meat and beans, saltines, orange drink, and five pieces of hard candy. Another work-out in the afternoon stacking ammo which we'll take out by truck tomorrow:.

Work goes on

Local support, ready to go & dressed for 100° weather

Chapter Twenty-three

MY BRUSH WITH DEATH... AND NOT FROM BOMBS

Days later, we were finishing off the dumps in and around Lae when I woke up one morning feeling awful, and some of the men at breakfast said, "You look terrible, Lieutenant!" So they took me over to the Australian field hospital where, sure enough, I was diagnosed with malaria. They popped me into bed and the sisters, who were the Australian nurses, not a religious group, took good care of me in the daytime. In the nighttime, they were hard to find.

The first night, I went into one of my high temperatures, the fever broke and I perspired gallons. So I got up and took a shower, and they were aghast. The sisters said, "You're not supposed to be out of bed!" and I said, "Well I couldn't find anybody who was there to sponge me down!"

The following morning, after the first night in the hospital, the Australian doctor in charge of the ward came in and said, "Good morning, Lieutenant, we didn't expect to see you today." And I said, "Captain, I felt too awful to have gone anyplace." He said, "I didn't mean that, we thought you were going to die last night." Interestingly, Julie had written some letters in January, all vaguely referring to, and sometimes spoken outright, of sickness and disease in New Guinea and how she prayed I'd avoided them and how she was sure I was down sick. Very, very interesting in view of the fact, a month later, it all came true. I think she's a little bit psychic.

When I began to recuperate, various Australian Military men—also patients recuperating, mostly from malaria—would come to my bed to play monopoly. I was still under mosquito netting as they didn't want "the new boy" re-infecting the others by mosquitoes having lunched on his blood.

The monopoly set was British, although the rules were the same. I had to get used to Mayfair and Park Lane instead of Boardwalk and Park Place. Then there were Picadilly, Leicester Square, and King's Cross station to name a few. When you went to jail, you were in the Gaol. One other oddity was the money was in dollars, not pounds. I invariably won my monopoly games and my Aussie opponent would leave my bedside muttering, "These Yankees! How could you ever take money from one of them?"

After about 15 days in the Australian field hospital, I lost a lot of weight because their idea of meals was stewed rabbit for one meal and tripe for the next, followed by stewed rabbit, then tripe. If a friendly sister hadn't provided me with some chocolate bars, I think I'd have starved to death. As it was, I was down to about 140 pounds when I came home, which was about 30 pounds under my normal weight. The doctors in the Australian 102nd Casualty Clearing Station, which is actually a hospital, thought that I should've been out of there within the normal 14 or 15 day period but my temperature zoomed up again to 104° and they realized that there was something else I might be carrying in my blood stream. It turned out that I had been bitten by a scrub-typhus tick and they had to go to work with different medicines to try to address the new infection. That took another three or four days, and I got out of there just as they were closing down the hospital and moving it back to Australia.

My three bomb disposal squad men had flown back to Batangas after finishing the job in that area, and I flew back shortly thereafter. Was this commendation worth the troubles and illness in New Guinea?

HEADQUARTERS BASE F
UNITED STATES ARMY FORCES WESTERN PACIFIC
Office of the Ordnance Officer

HWM/wsw
14 February 1946

SUBJECT: Commendation.

To: Commanding Officer, 208th Bomb Disposal Squad, APO 73.
(Through) Ordnance Officer, Base "R" , APO 73.

1. It is felt that recognition should be made of the excellent work done at this Base and Lae by all members of the 208th Bomb Disposal Squad, placed on temporary duty at this Base for the purpose of destroying dangerous ammunition.

2. Their devotion to the job at hand, ability to organize, supervise and instill confidence in the minds of the casual laborers unaccustomed to this dangerous work, was highly commendable and most gratifying to see. They fulfilled their mission with a superior type of efficiency.

ROBERT W. METCALF
Capt.
Ordnance Officer

When I got back to Batangas, we had to clear out the tents of the remnants of the first Filipino Bomb Disposal squad which had been occupying our area in the two months we had been gone.

At that time, I went into the hospital for a checkup and they found my blood was totally clean of parasites for both ailments. They pronounced me fit—though skinny. Corporal Shroeder shortly thereafter came down with malaria. His was the common type so they told him it would recur periodically for the next two or three years. I had been lucky, if you could call it that, in that I had malignant tertia malaria, which kills a high percentage of the soldiers who get it but, if one survives, it never recurs. And I've never had any recurrence of malaria.

Just before my orders came to leave because I had more than enough points, Sergeant Nanney went into the hospital with a temperature. I never found out what it was because I left before he was diagnosed but I'm pretty sure he had come down with malaria as well. Which meant that 3 out of 4 of us had gotten malaria in the New Guinea area, which is a pretty good batting average. The Ordnance Officer offered me a captaincy (which I should have had months before)[3] if I signed on for another six months. I told him that would do me little good because Julie would kill me when I got home. So, I declined and off I went.

3. As the song went, "Bless them all, bless them all, the long and the short and the tall. There'll be no promotion this side of the ocean, so cheer up my lads, bless them all."

Chapter Twenty-four

HOME AGAIN

I was driven to Manila with my valpak and my foot locker, and in due course, after a few days at a repple depple, I was assigned to the U.S.S. General William Weigel, a troop ship holding 10,000 troops. The ship was jam-packed with troops returning to the United States. We had three-decker bunks and two meals a day, but as there were poker games going on 24 hours a day, we didn't spend a lot of time in our bunks. And as we were going home, the lack of a third daily meal didn't bother us at all. I got into a poker game and was doing very well when I was approached by Major Al Lumley, who for years was the track coach at Amherst College, so I knew him from our pre-war days. He indicated that he had been tapped out at his poker game and asked, "Win, may I borrow 50 dollars?" I was happy to lend it to him. That night he must have won, because the next day he repaid me. I hear his luck went up and down on that trip, as it did for many of us. But the real luck was that we were on our way home. At the end of the voyage, he told me he had done very well and made several hundred dollars, quite a little nest egg coming out of a war!

I thought it was interesting to run into the Amherst track coach on our return trip. I was actually amazed at the number of people I'd met from my earlier life. From a Scout Master to my own father to a track coach from college. It **is** a small world. Al Lumley was an awfully nice guy, and we became good friends on the journey home. Coincidentally when my youngest daughter—born in 1949—moved to Amherst as an adult, she took me for a visit to a lilac farm. It was beautiful—and it was owned by Al Lumley. More than forty years after our trip home on the U.S.S. General William Weigel, Al and I were having drinks at his house, regaling each other with war stories.

U.S.S. General William Weigel AP-119

We left Manila on March 27, and the troop ship being fast, we were doing about 200 miles a day. One day, the ship's daily paper, the Weigel Decho, had a headline, "Demobilization halted: all discharges frozen." The daily progress chart showed the ship had turned and was heading back to Manila. This was a blow to all of us, until we finally realized the date was April 1 and this was a huge joke. We were still on our way home.

We hit the tail end of a typhoon and the ship was bobbing up and down like a cork, which didn't bother us when we were on deck, and didn't bother us when we were playing poker. We were too busy to notice. But if I went into my bunk or into the mess hall it was no fun at all. Very queasy. We finally outran that and April 11th we arrived in San Francisco. A band came out to greet us playing "Sentimental Journey," which is enough to make you cry after you had been overseas awhile.

I called Julie from San Francisco and, in the course of our conversation, she said, "Shave it off," referring to my bushy mustache. So I did, and my wife saw me only clean-shaven for the next sixty-four years, though as I write, I have, for the first time since that day, grown a mustache. It's a little greyer than the one I had in 1946, but I must say I look dapper! And Julie has not complained.

Next a long, crowded train trip to Fort Dix, N.J., where we were to be mustered out. I managed one trip to the Colonel's Scarsdale home where Julie was living with our two youngsters. I completely surprised her when I came in the front door. A lovely reunion as I hugged my three year-old daughter Frances and had my first look at my son Tom, now nearly one.

In the discharge process at Ft. Dix, I was asked if I wished to stay in the Army Reserve, which would entail two weeks training each year. I declined and signed a form to finalize my complete severance from the Military.

The W.A.C. (Women's Army Corps) captain who gave me my last interview tried hard to match my army experience with civilian occupations, but finally gave up on bomb disposal. "New York City police bomb squad? No? Good luck getting a job, Lieutenant."

When I took my physical exam to return to my position at MACY's, the only major change was in my hearing. No one thought of earmuffs or earplugs in WWII. So thousands of explosions effectively eliminated my hearing in the higher range of sounds.

Great to be back in Civilian life: an Easter egg hunt with Julie, Frances and Tom—they sleeveless and I in a heavy jacket and still cold—celebrating Tom's first birthday, finding out again the thousand reasons I married Julie five years earlier.

And that was the end of Win Firman's War. The bomb disposal man was home.

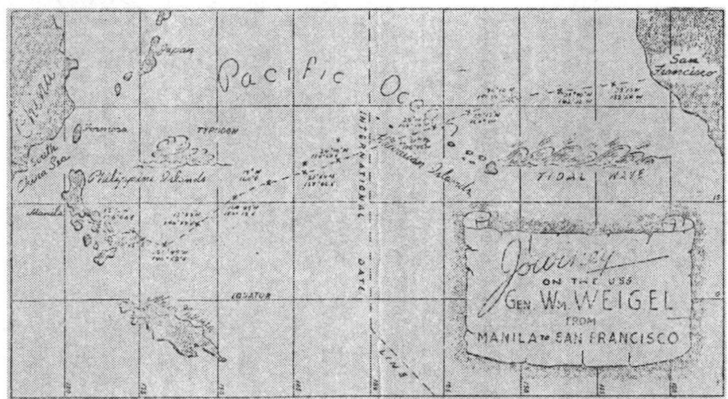

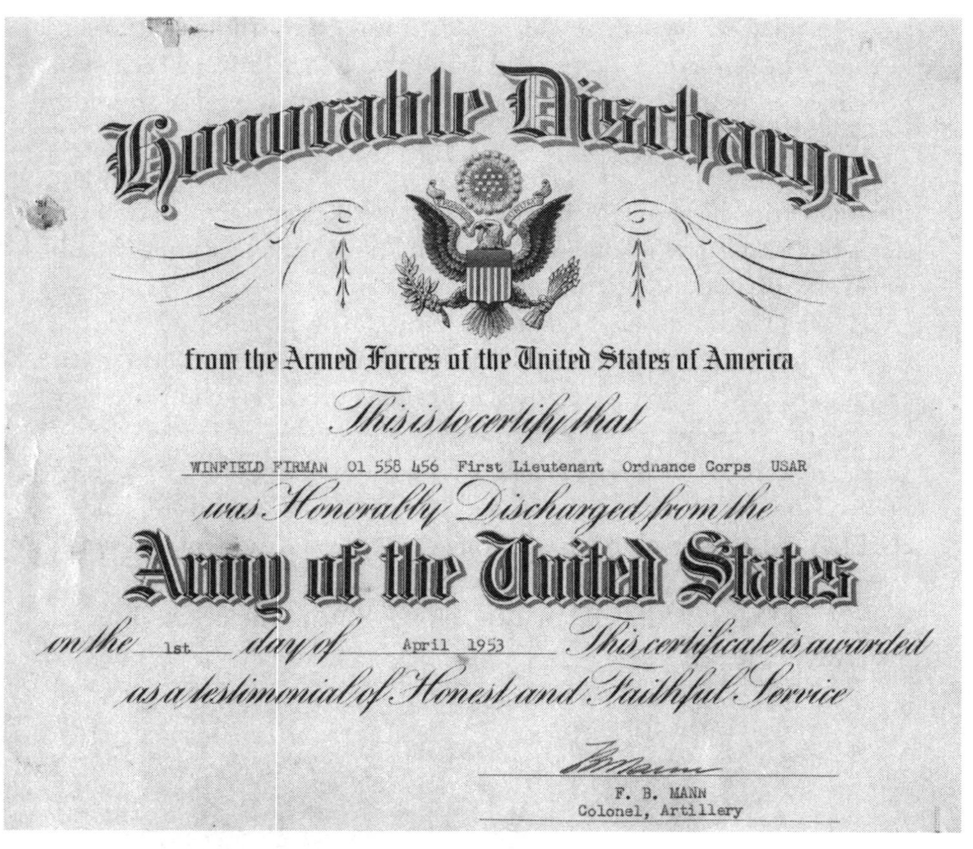

Honorable Discharge

from the Armed Forces of the United States of America

This is to certify that

WINFIELD FIRMAN 01 558 456 First Lieutenant Ordnance Corps USAR

was Honorably Discharged from the

Army of the United States

on the 1st day of April 1953 This certificate is awarded as a testimonial of Honest and Faithful Service

F. B. MANN
Colonel, Artillery

POSTSCRIPT

On May 11, 2010, a ninety-year old man, who has lived every one of his youthful dreams, works on his memoir. On the same day, the 111th Congress of the United States, passes Resolution 1294.

H.RES.1294

Title: ***Expressing support for designation of the first Saturday in May as National Explosive Ordnance Disposal Day to honor those who are serving and have served in the noble and self-sacrificing profession of Explosive Ordnance Disposal in the United States Armed Forces.***

This long-retired Bomb Disposal Officer appreciates that we have been noticed and salutes those who have continued and will continue through many difficult military engagements to lead the way as Bomb Disposal Personnel.

CPSIA information can be obtained
at www.ICGtesting.com
Printed in the USA
FFOW02n1800150514
5396FF